Dedication

To every young woman reading these pages,
This book is for you. It's for the girl who feels unseen, who wonders if she's worthy of love, or who feels trapped in the darkness of life's struggles. I want you to know that God sees you—exactly as you are. He knows every part of your story, and He loves you with a love that's deeper and more unshakable than you can even imagine.
As you journey through these pages, may you find healing and hope. May you discover the strength to break free from fear, shame, and doubt. And above all, may you learn to rest in the truth that you are loved beyond measure.
This is for you—the girl who is fighting, the girl who is healing, and the girl who is finding her way back to the light. You are not alone. You are loved. You are enough.
With all my love,
Angel

Table of Contents

Days 1-10: Finding Peace in His Love

1. ***Day 1:*** *Understanding God's Unfailing Love*
2. ***Day 2:*** *You Are Not Alone*
3. ***Day 3:*** *God's Promises for You*
4. ***Day 4:*** *Healing Begins with Trust*
5. ***Day 5:*** *Letting Go of Fear*
6. ***Day 6:*** *You Are Beautifully Made*
7. ***Day 7:*** *God's Love Never Fails*
8. ***Day 8:*** *Embracing Your Worth*
9. ***Day 9:*** *Holding on to Hope*
10. ***Day 10:*** *God's Peace for Your Heart*

Days 11-20: Growing Trust in God's Plan
11. ***Day 11:*** *Trusting God Through the Hard Times*
12. ***Day 12:*** *He Knows Your Heart*
13. ***Day 13:*** *Leaning on God in Prayer*
14. ***Day 14:*** *Embracing God's Timing*
15. ***Day 15:*** *The Strength in Your Weakness*
16. ***Day 16:*** *Walking by Faith, Not Sight*
17. ***Day 17:*** *Understanding God's Purpose for You*
18. ***Day 18:*** *Finding Peace in Surrender*
19. ***Day 19:*** *Trusting God with Your Future*
20. ***Day 20:*** *God's Plan is Greater Than Our Own*

Days 21-30: Embracing God's Grace and Love
21. ***Day 21:*** *Living in His Grace*
22. ***Day 22:*** *Unconditionally Loved by God*
23. ***Day 23:*** *The Joy of His Presence*
24. ***Day 24:*** *Understanding Your Identity in Christ*
25. ***Day 25:*** *God's Love Heals All Wounds*
26. ***Day 26:*** *Finding Freedom in His Grace*
27. ***Day 27:*** *You Are His Masterpiece*
28. ***Day 28:*** *God's Love Transforms You*
29. ***Day 29:*** *Embracing the Abundance of His Love*
30. ***Day 30:*** *Living a Life Overflowing with Love*

Day 31: Sharing God's Love with Others
31. ***Day 31:*** *Becoming a Vessel of Love*

Introduction

Hey, beautiful soul,

Welcome to Wings of Grace: A 31-Day Journey to Embrace God's Love and Heal Your Heart. I'm so glad you're here. If you're holding this journal, I believe God has a purpose for you in this moment—His love is waiting to wrap around you in ways you might not even expect.

Life can feel heavy sometimes, right? Like everything is coming at you all at once, and it's hard to keep your head above water. Maybe you're struggling with feeling lost, like you're not enough, or wondering if God really sees you. I want you to know this: His love is unshakable, no matter what you're going through. You are His precious daughter, and nothing can ever change that.

This journal is all about planting seeds of faith, self-worth, and hope in your heart. Over the next 31 days, we'll nurture those seeds together, letting God's light bring them to life. Like any growth process, it will take time, care, and trust. But as those seeds grow, you'll begin to see the first signs of the angel wings God has designed just for you.

This is just the beginning. In Part 2 of this journey, we'll focus on helping those wings take flight, guiding you to step into your role as an ambassador of God's love. But for now, this journal is about helping you see yourself the way God sees you—strong, beautiful, and deeply loved.

How This Journal Works

Each day is divided into two parts:

Morning:

Start your day with a personal note from me, a scripture from the New Testament, and a poem to connect with the day's theme. You'll find reflection questions to dig deeper into your heart and think about ways to share God's love with others. Then, you'll read a devotional thought to process it all, followed by a prayer and a journaling prompt to capture your thoughts and prayers.

Evening:

End your day with another personal note from me, an Old Testament scripture, and a guided poem for you to finish. The evening reflection questions will help you look back on how God's love showed up in your day and inspire you to share that love with others. Finally, you'll close with a prayer and a journaling prompt to reflect and prepare for tomorrow.

This journal is designed to be interactive—a place for you to reflect, create, and connect with God. Each page is your safe space to share what's on your heart, what you're wrestling with, or even what you're celebrating. Think of it like a diary with God. There's no right or wrong way to express yourself here. Be honest, be vulnerable, and know that God is always listening.

As you write, especially in the poetry sections, I encourage you to use a pencil. Poetry is about finding the right words that speak to your heart, and that might take some erasing and rewriting. It's all part of the process, and I'm excited for you to discover your own unique voice along the way.

A Journey Together

This journal is the first step in a journey to embrace God's love fully. By the end of these 31 days, my prayer is that you'll feel God's love in ways you've never experienced before—lifting your self-esteem, healing your heart, and preparing you for the next step.

So let's get started, one day at a time. Are you ready to take the first step? I'll be with you every step of the way, praying for you, cheering you on, and believing that you are exactly who God created you to be.

With love and prayers,
Angel

About Angel Schmid

Angel Schmid is an 18-year-old college student at TCC, studying arts and music. Her life is deeply rooted in her Christian faith, and through her music, writing, and personal story, she hopes to inspire and uplift young women who are facing life's toughest challenges. Angel's journey has been anything but perfect, but she's learned that God's love is the one thing that can restore even the deepest wounds—and that's exactly what she wants to share with others.

For years, Angel was caught in the darker side of the modeling industry, manipulated by those who took advantage of her and pushed her into situations that went against her Christian values. She found herself in an emotionally and physically scarred place, questioning her worth and feeling hopeless. It was during one of her darkest nights, lying in tears, that she mumbled a simple prayer: "God, do you still love me? I'm so sorry." This humble cry for help marked the turning point in her life—a moment when God's unconditional love broke through her fear and shame, reminding her that He had never left her side.

By God's grace, Angel found the strength to break free from the toxic environment she had been in. It wasn't easy, and it wasn't instant. There were times when she was still battling shame and self-doubt, but through it all, she discovered that God's love was constant, unchanging, and never-ending. She began to rebuild her life, rediscovering her identity in Christ and embracing the truth that her worth was found in His love, not in the world's expectations.

Angel wants other young women to know that healing is possible, no matter how far you've fallen. Her story isn't about being the perfect pastor's kid—it's about someone who has been through the mess and darkness, someone who has been broken but found wholeness in God's embrace. Angel is still on her journey, still healing, still learning, and still growing—but she's determined to share the love and grace she's received with others. She believes that no matter how deep you feel the struggle, God's love can lift you out of it.

You are not alone. God sees you, He knows you, and He calls you His own. His love is bigger than anything you've been through, and He will walk with you every step of the way. Wherever you are, remember: You are loved, you are enough, and healing is within reach.

With love and prayers,
Angel

How to Use This Journal

Hey beautiful soul, I'm so excited you're here, ready to embrace God's love in a deeper way! This journal is designed to help you grow, reflect, and connect with Him every single day. Here's how to use it:

1. ***Personal Note from Angel (Morning & Evening)***
   Each day begins and ends with a personal note from me. Read it to start or end your day, and let it inspire and encourage you. You're not alone in this journey—I'm cheering you on and praying for you as you take each step forward!
2. ***Scripture (Morning & Evening)***
   Take a moment to read the scripture for the day. Let these words settle in your heart, and think about how they speak to you today. God's Word is alive and ready to guide you, no matter where you are in life.
3. ***Poem (Morning)***
   Read the poem I've written for you. Let it fill your heart with hope and peace, and remind you of God's deep love for you. This is a time to let the words sink in and reflect on how they connect to your life.
4. ***Guided Poem (Evening)***
   Here's a guided poem for the evening. Read the first few lines, and then finish it with at least two lines of your own. Let your heart flow freely, and don't worry about making it perfect—just let your words reflect your true feelings and thoughts.
5. ***Reflection Questions (Morning & Evening)***
   Answer the reflection questions in one sentence each. The morning questions will help you reflect on how God's love is working in your life, and the evening ones will help you think about how you can share that love with others. Just let your answers flow naturally.
6. ***Devotional Thought (Morning & Evening)***
   After reading the devotional thought, take time to let it sink in. It's there to help you understand the scripture and poem on a deeper level and to show you how to live out God's love in everyday moments.
7. ***Prayer (Morning & Evening)***
   Each prayer starts with my words, but this is your time to talk to God. Finish it in your own words from your heart. Whether you need to pour out your feelings or simply sit in God's presence, He's always there for you, listening with love.
8. ***Journaling Prompt (Morning & Evening)***
   The journaling prompt is your chance to reflect and write what's on your heart. There's no right or wrong way to do this—just be honest and open with God. Write down your thoughts, feelings, prayers, or anything you feel led to share. Your voice matters.

By following these steps each day, you'll grow closer to God and experience His peace, love, and grace in ways you never imagined. I'm so proud of you for taking this step, and I'm here with you every day of this journey. You are so loved!

With all my love,
Angel

Day 1: Understanding God's Unfailing Love

Morning Entry

Personal Note from Angel:
Hey beautiful soul,
Welcome to Day 1 of our journey. I'm so excited to walk through this with you. Today, we're diving into one of the most powerful truths you'll ever encounter—God's unfailing love. Life can often make us feel alone, unsure, or even unworthy, but I want you to know today that God's love never wavers. He loves you deeply, beyond what you can even imagine. So let's open our hearts to His love and begin to embrace it fully.

Scripture (New Testament):
"But God demonstrates His own love for us in this: While we were still sinners, Christ died for us." — Romans 5:8

Poem:
God's love is a lighthouse shining bright,
A constant guide through the darkest night.
No mountain high, no valley low,
Can keep us from the love He'll always show.

When doubts surround, when fears invade,
His promises stand—they never fade.
In life or death, in joy or pain,
His steadfast love will ever remain.

Through storms that rage, through endless seas,
His love endures, a calming breeze.
His arms are wide, His heart is pure,
A love that heals, a love that's sure.

No chain can bind, no wall can block,
The endless love that He unlocks.
So rest in Him, let worries cease,
In His embrace, you'll find true peace.

Reflection Questions (Morning):

1. How does the knowledge of God's unfailing love make you feel today?

2. What is one way you can begin to experience or share God's love with others this morning?

Devotional Thought:
God's love is not something we have to earn, and it's not something that fades when we fall short. Romans 5:8 reminds us that God loved us even when we were far from Him—when we were broken and lost in sin. His love for you is constant and unchanging, regardless of the circumstances. Today, reflect on how God's love has been a steady force in your life. His love never abandons you, no matter what. Let this truth settle into your heart and know that it will never change.

Prayer:
Father, thank You for loving me with an unfailing love. Even when I fall short, You are there, embracing me with grace. Help me to truly understand the depth of Your love for me. I want to live today with the confidence that Your love will never fail. I trust in Your promises, and I know that You are always with me.

Journaling Prompt:
Reflect on a moment when you've felt God's love in a powerful way. How did it impact you, and how can you carry that feeling with you throughout the day? Write down your thoughts and anything that comes to mind as you reflect on His love.

Evening Entry

Personal Note from Angel:
Hey beautiful,
I hope your day was filled with moments where you felt God's love in a tangible way. As we end the day, I want to encourage you to reflect on how His love has shown up in your life today. Even in the hardest moments, His love is still there. It's always with you. Let's take this time to acknowledge it and give thanks.

Scripture (Old Testament):
"The Lord your God is with you, the Mighty Warrior who saves. He will take great delight in you; in His love He will no longer rebuke you, but will rejoice over you with singing." — Zephaniah 3:17

Guided Poem:

(Finish in your own words)
God's love is a shield, protecting me,
From the battles of life that I can't see.
His peace, a river, flowing wide,
He whispers, "Child, come and abide."

In moments of doubt, He's standing near,
His arms of grace, holding me here.
He leads me gently, through each night,
And fills my soul with endless light.

Reflection Questions (Evening):

1. How did God's love show up in your day today?

2. Who can you share God's love with tomorrow, and how will you do that?

Devotional Thought:
Zephaniah 3:17 beautifully describes how God rejoices over us with singing. Even when we're overwhelmed, God's love is a constant source of joy and peace. Tonight, reflect on how God has been present with you today—through challenges, victories, or quiet moments. His love is always there, cheering you on, even when you don't notice. Rest in the truth that God delights in you, and His love will always be with you.

Prayer:
Lord, thank You for filling me with Your love and joy today. I rest in knowing that Your love is unchanging, and that You delight in me. Help me to carry Your love into tomorrow, and to share it with those who need it most. I trust that Your love will guide me through all things.

Journaling Prompt:
Take a moment to reflect on how you felt God's love today. What are you thankful for? What did you learn about God's love that you want to carry into tomorrow? Write down your thoughts and how you'll embrace His love in the coming days.

Day 2: You Are Not Alone

Morning Entry

Personal Note from Angel: Hey, sweet girl! I want you to know right now that you are not alone. Whatever you're walking through today, God is with you every step of the way. He's holding you close, even in the moments when you feel unsure or overwhelmed. I've been there, and I want you to remember that His love surrounds you, even in your darkest hours. Lean on Him, and you'll see He's been beside you all along.

Scripture (New Testament):
"For I am with you, and no one will attack you to harm you, for I have many in this city who are my people."
— Acts 18:10 (ESV)

Poem:
You are not alone, my dear,
Though the storm clouds gather near.
His presence fills the space around,
In every silence, He's still found.
When you feel the weight of night,
He'll be your ever-present light.
The world may seem a lonely place,
But God will always guard your space.
He whispers softly in the dark,
Calling you to feel His spark.
When shadows loom and hearts may break,
His love is strong, for your sake.
Stand firm, for you are not alone,
His love has made you fully known.

Reflection Questions (Morning):

1. How does it feel to know that God is always with you, especially in your hardest moments?

2. In what ways can you lean into God's presence today, trusting that you are not alone?

Devotional Thought:
It's so easy to feel isolated when life gets tough. But God's word tells us over and over that He is with us. His love isn't distant or detached; it's near, close enough to comfort us when we need it most. No matter where you are or what you're going through, God's presence is constant. When the world feels overwhelming, remember that He has already placed His love and peace within your reach. You are never alone, and you don't have to face anything without Him by your side.

Prayer:
Lord, I thank You for being with me through every moment of my day. Even when I can't feel You, I trust that You are near. Help me to rest in Your presence and lean on You when things get hard. Show me Your love today, and remind me that I am never alone. Amen.

Journaling Prompt:
Take a moment to reflect on a time when you felt God's presence close to you. What did that moment teach you about His faithfulness? Write a letter to God expressing your gratitude for always being with you, no matter the circumstances.

Evening Entry

Personal Note from Angel:
As you end your day, I hope you can rest in the peace that God is always with you, watching over you as you sleep. Take a moment to reflect on His love that has been with you throughout this day. No matter what the day brought, you are never far from His heart. I'm so proud of you for trusting Him in each moment.

Scripture (Old Testament):
"The Lord your God is with you, the Mighty Warrior who saves. He will take great delight in you; in His love He will no longer rebuke you, but will rejoice over you with singing."
— Zephaniah 3:17 (NIV)

Guided Poem:

(Finish in your own words)
I rest tonight in God's embrace,
A Mighty Warrior, full of grace.
He guards my heart with tender care,
And fills my soul with love so rare.
His love is strong, it will not fade,
A shelter in the storm, well laid.
No fear will take away my peace,
For in His love, I find release.
I feel His presence, calm and near,
And know that I am free from fear.

Reflection Questions (Evening):

1. How did you experience God's love today? How did it show up in your life?

2. How can you share that love with someone else tomorrow? Who in your life needs to know they are not alone?

Devotional Thought:
God's love is not just a passive presence; it's active, fighting for us, singing over us, and protecting us in every moment. Zephaniah reminds us that God delights in us, even when we don't feel worthy. His love doesn't change with our circumstances, and it never fails. Tonight, rest in the knowledge that His love is constant, and you can trust in His strength to carry you through every trial.

Prayer:
God, thank You for being a Mighty Warrior who is always with me. As I rest tonight, I trust that Your peace surrounds me. Help me to feel Your delight in me, even when I can't see it. Show me ways to reflect Your love to others tomorrow. Amen.

Journaling Prompt:
Take a few minutes to list five things you're grateful for from today. Consider how God's love showed up in each one. Write a letter to God, thanking Him for His constant presence in your life and asking Him to help you share His love with others.

Day 3: God's Promises for You

Morning Entry
Personal Note from Angel:
Good morning, beautiful soul! Today, I want to remind you of the promises God has made to you, and how those promises never change, no matter what you face. Sometimes life gets overwhelming, and it can feel like things won't get better, but God's promises are unshakable. He's with you every step of the way, and He has incredible plans for your life. Let today be a reminder of His love and faithfulness toward you, no matter the circumstances. You are never alone.

Scripture (New Testament):
"For all the promises of God find their Yes in him. That is why it is through him that we utter our Amen to God for his glory."
— 2 Corinthians 1:20 (ESV)

Poem:
God's promises are like morning light,
Shining brightly through the night,
A promise of love that never fades,
A hope that through the storms, cascades.

He promises peace that fills the soul,
A balm for hearts that make us whole,
Through every trial, He will guide,
And in His arms, we will reside.

No fear can steal His steadfast grace,
His love will hold us in its place,
So when the world feels far away,
Remember, His promises are here to stay.

Reflection Questions (Morning):

1. How does it feel to know that God's promises are unchanging and always available to you?

2. In what areas of your life do you need to lean on God's promises today?

Devotional Thought:
God's promises are a powerful source of comfort and strength. No matter what you're going through, God's Word reminds us that He has promised to be with us through it all. When we feel lost or uncertain, we can trust that He is guiding us and working for our good. Take time today to reflect on those promises, knowing that His love and faithfulness are unshakable.

Prayer:
Dear Lord, thank You for Your incredible promises. I trust that You are faithful and that Your love will never leave me. Help me to hold on to Your promises today, especially when I feel uncertain or afraid. I know You are with me, guiding me every step of the way. Amen.

Journaling Prompt:
Take a moment to write about a time when you experienced God's faithfulness. Reflect on how His promises were evident in that moment. How can you carry that truth into today?

Evening Entry
Personal Note from Angel:
As the day comes to a close, I want you to know that God's promises are still true, even in the quiet moments. No matter how your day went, He is with you, offering peace and rest. Tonight, take a deep breath and let His presence calm your heart. Tomorrow is a new day, full of fresh hope and His unchanging love. You are loved, and you are enough.

Scripture (Old Testament):
"For the mountains may depart
and the hills be removed,
but my steadfast love shall not depart from you,
and my covenant of peace shall not be removed,"
says the Lord, who has compassion on you.
— Isaiah 54:10 (ESV)

Guided Poem:

(Finish in your own words)
God's love is steadfast, always near,
A promise to wipe away every tear.
Through every storm, His love remains,
And in His presence, joy sustains.

His peace will fill your heart tonight,
A refuge of grace, gentle and bright.
His love will never leave your side,
And with Him, you'll forever abide.

Reflection Questions (Evening):

1. How did you experience God's promises throughout the day?

2. How can you share God's promises with others tomorrow, offering them the same hope and peace He's given you?

Devotional Thought:
As you reflect on the day, remember that God's love and peace are never-ending. No matter what challenges you may face, His promises hold true. Tonight, take comfort in knowing that His love will never leave you, and He will always be there to guide you. Trust in His faithfulness as you rest.

Prayer:
Lord, thank You for Your steadfast love and for the promises You've made to me. I rest in Your peace tonight, knowing that You are always near. Help me to trust in Your promises more fully each day. I am so grateful for Your presence in my life. Amen.
(Leave space for personalization)

Journaling Prompt:
Take a moment to reflect on how you saw God's promises in action today. Write down one thing you are grateful for and one way you will share God's love with others tomorrow.

Here's Day 4, "Healing Begins with Trust,

Morning Entry:

Personal Note from Angel
Good morning, beautiful soul! Healing is a journey, and it starts with trust. I know it's not always easy to trust, especially when life feels broken. But trust is the first step towards the peace and restoration God promises us. As you begin this day, remember that healing is already happening inside of you, even if you can't see it yet. God's love is healing you, piece by piece.

Scripture (New Testament)
"Trust in the Lord with all your heart, and do not lean on your own understanding. In all your ways acknowledge Him, and He will make straight your paths." — Proverbs 3:5-6 (ESV)

Poem
When your heart is heavy and filled with doubt,
Trust in the Lord, He'll show you a way out.
In His arms, you'll find your peace,
A promise that will never cease.
Healing begins where trust is found,
In His love, you are safe and sound.
No need to fear or fight alone,
He'll lead you to a place called home.
Your journey to wholeness starts today,
Trust in His love, and He'll show the way.
When you trust, healing can unfold,
In His embrace, you'll be made whole.

Reflection Questions (Morning)

1. In what area of your life is God calling you to trust Him more fully?

2. How can you surrender your understanding to His guidance today?

Devotional Thought
Healing requires vulnerability and trust. When we release our need to control every situation and place our trust in God, healing begins to take root. The path may not always be clear, but God promises that when we trust Him with all our hearts, He will guide us through the journey. It's not about having all the answers but about taking one step at a time with Him.

Prayer
Dear God, thank You for the healing You offer. I trust that You are working in my heart and my life, even when I can't see the changes yet. Help me let go of my fears and fully surrender to Your love. Teach me to trust You more deeply today and every day. In Jesus' name, Amen.

Journaling Prompt
Think about an area in your life where you're struggling to trust God. Write a prayer asking Him to help you release control and trust Him more fully. Reflect on any steps you can take today to surrender to His guidance.

Evening Entry:

Personal Note from Angel
As the day comes to a close, take a moment to breathe and relax. Healing takes time, and it's okay if you don't have all the answers today. I've learned that God's healing often happens in small, quiet moments. As you reflect on your day, remember that trust is the foundation of healing, and each day you trust Him more, He's working in your heart.

Scripture (Old Testament)
"He heals the brokenhearted and binds up their wounds." — Psalm 147:3 (ESV)

Guided Poem

(Finish in your own words)
In the quiet of the night,
God's healing love is shining bright.
He mends the broken, hearts of stone,
And gives the weary a place called home.
With gentle hands, He holds us near,
Wiping away each doubt and fear.
He binds our wounds, heals our pain,
And brings us joy to live again.
[Your Turn]

Reflection Questions (Evening)

1. How did you see God's healing work in your life today?

2. Is there someone you can reach out to and share God's healing love with tomorrow?

Devotional Thought
The promise of God's healing is real. Whether it's emotional wounds, physical pain, or spiritual struggles, God is the healer of all things. When we trust Him, He restores and makes us whole. Let tonight be a reminder that God is working in your life, healing and restoring you from the inside out. Rest in His love and know that He's not finished with you yet.

Prayer
God, thank You for Your healing hands that work in my life. I'm so grateful that You are healing my heart and my wounds. I trust that You are always working, even when I can't see the results. Please continue to guide me on my healing journey. In Jesus' name, Amen.

Journaling Prompt
Reflect on any areas where you are still waiting for healing. Write a letter to God, expressing your hopes and your trust in His perfect timing.

Day 5: Letting Go of Fear

Morning Entry

Personal Note from Angel
Hey there, beautiful soul. I know that fear can feel like an overwhelming weight, but I want to remind you today that God is bigger than any fear you might face. When we let go of the fear that holds us back, we make room for God's perfect love to fill our hearts. Remember, He's right there with you in the midst of the struggles, ready to give you peace and strength. You don't have to do it alone—trust Him to carry you through today.

Scripture (New Testament)
"There is no fear in love. But perfect love drives out fear, because fear has to do with punishment. The one who fears is not made perfect in love." – 1 John 4:18

Poem
Fear may whisper in your ear,
A shadow that won't disappear.
But love is louder, love is strong,
A song that guides you all day long.
Perfect love, from God above,
Is here to chase the fear we've shoved.
When you let go, and trust His hand,
You'll find His peace in every land.
So breathe it in, and let it go,
The fear will fade, and love will grow.
His love is all you need to fight,
And walk in freedom, full of light.

Reflection Questions (Morning)

1. How does the fear I'm carrying today affect my relationship with God?

2. What is one thing I can do today to trust God more and let go of fear?

Devotional Thought

Fear can often hold us back, keeping us from stepping into the fullness of God's plan for us. But when we understand that His love is perfect and strong, fear has no place in our hearts. We are made for freedom, and God's love is the key to breaking every chain of fear. Today, let His perfect love remind you that no matter what you face, you are safe and secure in His care.

Prayer

God, thank You for Your perfect love that drives out fear. Help me to trust You completely today and to let go of anything that is holding me back. I know that with You by my side, I don't have to be afraid. Thank You for Your peace and strength that fills my heart. I'm ready to walk in Your freedom. Amen.

Journaling Prompt

Take a moment to write down what fears you are holding onto. Ask God to help you release them today, and list the things that bring you peace and comfort. What is one step you can take today to choose trust over fear?

Evening Entry

Personal Note from Angel
As the day comes to a close, I want you to take a deep breath and remember how far you've come today. You've faced your fears and trusted God to lead you through, and that's something to be proud of. Rest now, knowing that His love is constant and unshakable, and He is always with you, even in the quiet moments. Let His peace fill your heart as you prepare for a peaceful night of rest.

Scripture (Old Testament)
"The Lord is my light and my salvation—whom shall I fear? The Lord is the stronghold of my life—of whom shall I be afraid?" – Psalm 27:1

Guided Poem

(Finish in your own words)
Fear once ruled, but now I see,
The strength of God is setting me free.
His light is bright, His love is strong,
And in His presence, I belong.
No more chains, no more fright,
His love fills me with endless light.
I trust in Him, my Savior true,
And in His strength, I will breakthrough.

Reflection Questions (Evening)

1. How have I seen God's love helping me to overcome fear today?

2. In what ways can I share the peace I've experienced with someone else?

Devotional Thought
As the day comes to an end, take a moment to reflect on how God's light and love have led you through. He is your salvation and your stronghold, and there's nothing to fear when you are in His hands. Trust in His love to carry you through every fear, and know that His peace will remain with you, even in the darkest times. Rest well, for tomorrow is another day to walk in His freedom.

Prayer
Lord, thank You for being my light and my salvation. Tonight, I rest in the knowledge that Your love will guide me through every fear and challenge. Help me to trust You even more tomorrow and share the peace You've given me with others. Thank You for being my constant strength. Amen.

Journaling Prompt
Reflect on today's theme of letting go of fear. Write a letter to God, thanking Him for His love and asking for His continued strength to overcome any fears in your life. What has been your biggest takeaway from today's reflections?

Day 6: You Are Beautifully Made

Morning Entry

Personal Note from Angel
Good morning, beautiful! I want you to start your day by looking in the mirror and seeing yourself the way God sees you—perfectly made and loved beyond measure. It's easy to forget this truth when we feel insecure or unsure, but remember, you are God's masterpiece. He created you with a purpose, and every part of you is a reflection of His love. Take today as a reminder that you are more than enough, just as you are. Let's embrace the day knowing that we are beautifully made by our Creator.

Scripture (New Testament)
"So God created mankind in his own image, in the image of God he created them; male and female he created them."
—Genesis 1:27

Poem
You are made in His image,
A reflection of love so pure,
Each detail He carefully crafted,
A masterpiece meant to endure.
Your beauty shines from within,
In every smile, every tear,
A heart that holds His endless grace,
And love that banishes fear.
From the top of your head to your toes,
Every part of you, divinely planned,
A living work of art that grows,
Held gently in God's loving hand.

Reflection Questions (Morning)

1. How do you see yourself when you think about being made in God's image?

2. What areas of your life can you embrace more fully as part of God's beautiful design for you?

Devotional Thought
The truth is, God made you exactly the way He wanted you. Every feature, every characteristic, every part of you was carefully designed by Him. When we realize that we are fearfully and wonderfully made, we can begin to embrace our uniqueness and walk in confidence. God's love for you is the foundation of your beauty, and this love is what gives you strength, joy, and purpose. Your beauty shines brightest when you live out His love with courage and grace.

Prayer
Dear God,
Thank You for making me in Your image, for creating me with purpose and love. I sometimes forget how beautifully I am made, but today, I choose to see myself through Your eyes. Help me to embrace every part of who I am, knowing that I am fearfully and wonderfully made. Thank You for Your love that never fails.

Journaling Prompt
Take a moment to reflect on the ways you are beautifully made by God. Write down three things you love about yourself, remembering that these qualities are gifts from Him. Also, think about how you can embrace these traits more fully today in your interactions and in the way you see yourself.

Evening Entry

Personal Note from Angel
As you prepare to end your day, I want to remind you that your beauty is not just in your appearance, but in the love you share with others. You are a reflection of God's love, and everything you do today was touched by His grace. Rest tonight knowing that you are loved just as you are, and there is nothing more you need to do to be worthy of His love. You are enough, and tomorrow is another chance to walk in that beauty.

Scripture (Old Testament)
"I praise you because I am fearfully and wonderfully made; your works are wonderful, I know that full well."
—Psalm 139:14

Guided Poem

(Finish in your own words)
God made me perfect, one of a kind,
A creation so beautiful, so divinely designed.
In His hands, I am whole,
A reflection of love, body and soul.
Each part of me shines with grace,
A masterpiece full of God's embrace.
My heart is filled with His love and care,
Knowing He's always there.

Reflection Questions (Evening)

1. How did you see God's love reflected in your actions today?

2. How can you share this love with others tomorrow?

Devotional Thought
Psalm 139 beautifully reminds us that we are wonderfully made, a living testament to God's creativity and love. As we reflect on this truth, it encourages us to embrace our identity in Christ fully. In a world that often tries to define us by external standards, we can rest in knowing that God has already defined us as His beautiful creation. Tonight, know that your worth is unshakable, and His love never changes.

Prayer
Dear God,
Thank You for creating me with such love and care. Tonight, I rest in the truth that I am fearfully and wonderfully made. Help me to see myself as You see me, and to share Your love with others in all I do. I am grateful for Your constant presence in my life.

Journaling Prompt
As you close your day, think about one way you shared God's love with someone today. How did it make you feel? Write about how you can continue to share His love in your actions and words tomorrow.

Day 7: God's Love Never Fails

Morning Entry

Personal Note from Angel:
Good morning, beautiful soul! Today, I want you to know that no matter what challenges you face, God's love will never fail you. There have been times when I've felt completely overwhelmed, but I've found peace in knowing that God's love is constant and unchanging. It holds me up, even on the hardest days, and I know it's holding you too. As you move through this day, remember that His love surrounds you, no matter what happens. Let His love fill your heart, knowing it will always remain.

Scripture (New Testament):
"For I am sure that neither death nor life, nor angels nor rulers, nor things present nor things to come, nor powers, nor height nor depth, nor anything else in all creation, will be able to separate us from the love of God in Christ Jesus our Lord."
— Romans 8:38-39

Poem:
God's love never fails, it stands so strong,
A perfect promise, forever long.
Through every trial, through every fear,
His love remains, always near.
No height, no depth, no wind, no storm,
Can tear apart what He's sworn.
His love is constant, pure, and true,
A shelter strong, forever new.
Through all the chaos, we find His peace,
In His embrace, our worries cease.
No circumstance can take away,
The love He gives, every day.

Reflection Questions (Morning):

1. How do you feel knowing that nothing can separate you from God's love?

2. In what areas of your life do you need to experience His unshakable love today?

Devotional Thought:
God's love is not dependent on our circumstances. It doesn't change with the seasons of our life; it remains steady and unyielding. When we struggle, when we doubt, or when we feel weak, His love is there to lift us up. Romans 8:38-39 reminds us that His love is inseparable. No matter what we face, we are always held by His everlasting love. Let that truth sink deep into your heart today.

Prayer:
Heavenly Father, thank You for Your endless love. I'm so grateful that nothing can take me away from Your arms. Please help me to remember this truth when I feel alone or overwhelmed. Remind me that You are always with me, holding me close. Let Your love fill my heart today.

Journaling Prompt:
Take a moment to reflect on God's love for you. Write down 3 things you are grateful for today that show His love in your life. Let your heart overflow with thanksgiving as you see the ways He cares for you.

Evening Entry

Personal Note from Angel:
As your day winds down, I hope you can feel God's love wrapping around you like a warm blanket. His love has been with you through each step of today, and it will continue to carry you through tomorrow. Rest easy knowing that nothing can shake His hold on your heart. Whatever you faced today, remember His love has been constant through it all. I'm praying for peace over your night and strength for tomorrow.

Scripture (Old Testament):
"The Lord your God is with you, the Mighty Warrior who saves. He will take great delight in you; in his love he will no longer rebuke you, but will rejoice over you with singing."
— Zephaniah 3:17

Guided Poem:

(Finish in your own words)
His love is strong, it never fails,
Through every storm, through all our trials,
He carries us when we cannot stand,
With His mighty, gentle hand.
When we falter, He stays near,
And wipes away our every tear.
His love sings over us so sweet,
A melody that makes us complete.

Reflection Questions (Evening):

1. How did you experience God's love today?

2. Who can you reach out to and share the comfort of God's love with tomorrow?

Devotional Thought:
As the day ends, remember that God delights in you. His love is not just a passive feeling; it's an active force that rejoices over you. In Zephaniah 3:17, we see a picture of God's love that sings over us—filling us with joy, peace, and strength. As we rest tonight, we can trust that He is rejoicing over us, just as we rejoice in His love.

Prayer:
Lord, thank You for this day and for Your constant, unchanging love. I rest in the truth that You delight in me and that Your love will never fail. Please continue to comfort me with Your presence and help me share Your love with others. I am so grateful for Your peace.

Journaling Prompt:
Before you close your eyes tonight, think of someone who might need to feel God's love tomorrow. Write a prayer or a note of encouragement for them. Let your heart be a vessel for His love.

Day 8: Embracing Your Worth

Morning Entry

Personal Note from Angel *Good morning, beautiful! Today is a new day to embrace who you truly are—worthy, loved, and cherished by God. Sometimes, we forget just how precious we are in His eyes. I've been there, feeling unsure, but remembering God's love for me always helped me find my worth again. Know that He sees you, He knows you, and He delights in you, just as you are. I pray that today, you feel His love in a fresh way, reminding you that you are more than enough in His eyes.*

Scripture (New Testament) *"For we are God's masterpiece. He has created us anew in Christ Jesus, so we can do the good things he planned for us long ago."*
— Ephesians 2:10 (NLT)

Poem
You are more than just a face in the crowd,
A masterpiece created, uniquely proud.
With every breath, you hold a story untold,
A love that's worth more than the world's gold.
You're chosen, cherished, deeply seen,
Wrapped in grace, a love serene.
In your flaws, His beauty shines bright,
His love makes you radiant in the darkest night.
Embrace the truth, hold it tight,
You are His, and He calls you right.
Don't doubt your worth, don't second guess,
You're His masterpiece, nothing less.
He's planned your path, He's made you whole,
You're a living story of love, heart, and soul.

Reflection Questions (Morning)

1. How do you currently see your worth in God's eyes?

2. In what areas of your life can you more fully embrace the love and value God has given you?

Devotional Thought
God created you with intention and love. When He looks at you, He sees beauty, purpose, and potential. In a world that often makes us feel small or unimportant, it's easy to forget that we are God's masterpiece. But this scripture reminds us that we are not accidents—we are designed by a loving Creator with a unique plan. Today, take time to reflect on that and let it fill you with confidence and peace. Embrace your worth as a beloved daughter of God, created for His purpose.

Prayer
Heavenly Father,
Thank You for creating me with such love and purpose. Help me to see myself through Your eyes today. When I struggle with doubt or insecurity, remind me that I am Your masterpiece. Fill my heart with the peace and confidence that comes from knowing You love me unconditionally. I trust in Your plan for my life and embrace the worth You've given me.

Journaling Prompt
Today, write a letter to yourself from God. Imagine that He is speaking directly to you, telling you how He sees you and how much He loves you. Let this be a reminder of your worth and identity in Him.

Evening Entry

Personal Note from Angel
As you wind down today, I hope you're feeling encouraged about your worth and the love God has for you. I know it's easy to get caught up in the busyness of life, but tonight I want to remind you to rest in the truth of who you are in Christ. You are loved beyond measure, and tomorrow is another opportunity to live in that truth. May you sleep peacefully, knowing that you are fully known and deeply cherished by God.

Scripture (Old Testament)
"The Lord your God is with you, the Mighty Warrior who saves. He will take great delight in you; in His love He will no longer rebuke you, but will rejoice over you with singing."
— Zephaniah 3:17 (NIV)

Guided Poem

(Finish in your own words)
You are not forgotten, never alone,
In His heart, you've always had a home.
His love for you is like a song,
Singing your worth all day long.
No matter the trials, no matter the pain,
His love for you will always remain.
Let His joy and peace surround,
As His love lifts you off the ground.

Reflection Questions (Evening)

1. How have you experienced God's love today?

2. .In what ways can you share God's love with someone else tomorrow?

Devotional Thought
As we reflect on the evening, take comfort in knowing that God delights in you. His love is not conditional or fleeting—it's everlasting. The God who created the stars, who parted the seas, is also the God who rejoices over you with singing. Let that truth settle in your heart tonight and bring you peace. Tomorrow is a new day, and God's love will be with you every step of the way.

Prayer
Dear God,
Thank You for the reminder of Your constant love and delight in me. I am so grateful that You see me as I am, and still You rejoice over me with joy. Tonight, I rest in Your love, knowing that I am cherished by the Creator of the universe. Help me to sleep in peace, trusting that You will be with me tomorrow, just as You are with me now.

Journaling Prompt
Reflect on the moments today when you felt God's love or peace. Write about how you can share that love with others tomorrow, whether through kindness, prayer, or simply being present.

Day 9: Holding on to Hope

Morning Entry

Personal Note from Angel:
Good morning, sweet soul! I know life can sometimes feel overwhelming, and it's easy to lose sight of hope. But I want to remind you that God's love is never far away, even in the hardest moments. Take a deep breath and know that hope is always present in the midst of trials. He sees you, He loves you, and He will carry you through. As you go about your day, hold on to that hope, and let it give you strength.

Scripture (New Testament):
"We have this hope as an anchor for the soul, firm and secure." – Hebrews 6:19

Poem:
Hope is the anchor in the storm,
A light that shines, pure and warm.
Through winds that howl, through waves that crash,
It holds us steady, despite the clash.
A whisper soft, a steady hand,
Guiding us through this weary land.
When doubt tries to steal our way,
Hope stands tall, leading the day.
With every step, it calls our name,
A promise that will never change.
Hold tight to hope, let it grow,
In His love, we'll always know.

Reflection Questions (Morning):

1. How does holding on to hope change the way you face challenges in your life?

2. What area of your life do you need God to anchor you in today?

Devotional Thought:
Hope is the thread that connects us to God's promises. No matter what you're facing today, know that God has given you an anchor in Jesus. Just as a ship is held firm in the storm by its anchor, you too can remain strong in the midst of life's difficulties. Hope doesn't mean the absence of struggles; it means that God is with you through them. Hold on to hope today—it's a reminder of God's unshakable faithfulness.

Prayer:
Father God, thank You for being my anchor in every storm. When life feels uncertain, help me to hold on to the hope that You are with me. I trust in Your love and Your faithfulness. Please give me the strength to keep moving forward, knowing that You will never let me go. I lift my heart to You today, trusting in Your hope.

Journaling Prompt:
Take a moment to write down any areas in your life where you need hope right now. Ask God to fill you with His peace and confidence, and trust that He is in control. How can you be more intentional about holding on to hope today?

Evening Entry

Personal Note from Angel:
As you wind down tonight, take a deep breath and reflect on the hope you've held on to today. It's been a day of trusting, and no matter what came your way, you've made it through. I hope you can feel God's peace surrounding you. No matter the trials you face, hope always remains. Rest tonight knowing that tomorrow is a new day to walk in His light.

Scripture (Old Testament):
"But those who hope in the Lord will renew their strength. They will soar on wings like eagles; they will run and not grow weary, they will walk and not be faint." – Isaiah 40:31

Guided Poem:

(Finish in your own words)
Hope is like the eagle's flight,
Soaring high in the morning light.
Above the clouds, above the storm,
It carries us, keeps us warm.
When we are weak, it makes us strong,
A melody, a perfect song.
In moments of doubt, we stand tall,
Our hope in God, the One who calls.

Reflection Questions (Evening):

1. How have you shared God's hope with someone today?

2. How can you offer hope to others in the coming days?

Devotional Thought:
As the day comes to a close, remember that hope isn't just for you—it's something to be shared. The hope you hold onto can be a light to others, showing them that God's love is unwavering. Just as He renews your strength, He can use you to help renew others' strength as well. Tonight, rest in the truth that God is your hope, and He's working in you and through you to share that hope with the world.

Prayer:
Lord, thank You for being the hope that sustains me. As I reflect on the day, I am reminded that You are always near, always faithful. Help me to share the hope I have in You with others, and let Your peace fill my heart tonight. I trust that You are at work in me and through me. Thank You for Your unending love and hope.

Journaling Prompt:
Reflect on the ways you've seen hope today. What blessings have you experienced, even in the small moments? Write a letter to God, expressing gratitude for the hope He's given you and how you've seen it at work in your life.

Day 10: God's Peace for Your Heart

Morning Entry

Personal Note from Angel
Good morning, sweet friend! I'm so glad we get to walk through this day together. Sometimes, life can feel so heavy, and we can forget that God's peace is always available to us. Today, I want to remind you that His peace isn't about everything being perfect but knowing that He is with us in every moment. Take a deep breath and trust that God's peace can cover you, no matter what you're facing today. You are not alone.

Scripture (New Testament)
"Peace I leave with you; my peace I give you. I do not give to you as the world gives. Do not let your hearts be troubled and do not be afraid."
—John 14:27 (NIV)

Poem
In the quiet of the morning light,
I find a peace that feels so right.
A stillness deep within my soul,
A gentle calm that makes me whole.
No fear can stay, no worry last,
For God's own peace is here, so vast.
It wraps me up and holds me tight,
A shelter in the darkest night.
This peace, a gift from heaven's hand,
Guides me through life's shifting sand.
In every step, I'll trust and see,
His peace will always set me free.

Reflection Questions (Morning)

1. How does God's peace make you feel as you start your day?

2. In what areas of your life do you need to invite God's peace more fully?

Devotional Thought
The peace that God offers isn't like the world's peace, which often depends on our circumstances. God's peace is constant and unshakable, and it comes to us as a gift. No matter what you're facing, His peace can calm your heart and mind. It's not about the absence of trouble, but the presence of God in the midst of it. Today, remember that His peace is available to you, regardless of your circumstances.

Prayer
Lord, I thank You for the peace that You give, a peace that surpasses all understanding. I ask that You fill my heart with this peace today. Help me to let go of my worries and trust that You are with me in every moment. I know that with You, I don't have to be afraid. Thank You for Your constant love and care.

Journaling Prompt
Take a moment to reflect on the areas of your life where you need God's peace. Write down what you're holding onto, and ask God to fill those spaces with His peace. How can you allow His peace to guide you through today?

Evening Entry

Personal Note from Angel
As the day comes to a close, I hope you're feeling the warmth of God's peace surrounding you. Tonight, as you reflect on all that's happened today, remember that peace doesn't disappear when the challenges come. It's always there, waiting for you to invite it in. Whatever struggles or worries you faced today, rest assured that God's peace is still with you, holding you close.

Scripture (Old Testament)
"You will keep in perfect peace those whose minds are steadfast, because they trust in you."
—Isaiah 26:3 (NIV)

Guided Poem

(Finish in your own words)
As the day fades into night,
God's peace fills me, calm and bright.
I feel His love, His steady hand,
Guiding me to a place so grand.
In His presence, all fear departs,
Leaving peace to fill my heart.
I close my eyes, and still I see...
His peace surrounds and comforts me.

Reflection Questions (Evening)

1. How did God's peace show up in your life today?

2. In what ways can you share God's peace with others tomorrow?

Devotional Thought
Isaiah reminds us that peace comes when we trust in God. Our minds can become overwhelmed by life's noise and distractions, but when we focus on God, His perfect peace fills our hearts. Tonight, take a moment to quiet your thoughts and rest in the assurance that God is holding you. You can trust Him, and He will keep you in peace.

Prayer
Father, thank You for Your peace that has been with me today. As I rest, I ask that You calm my heart and mind, and help me to feel Your presence in every moment. May Your peace continue to surround me as I sleep, and may I wake refreshed and ready to share Your peace with others.

Journaling Prompt
Write down a few ways you experienced peace today, and thank God for those moments. Consider how you can invite more of God's peace into your life tomorrow, and think about how you might share that peace with someone else.

Day 11: Trusting God Through the Hard Times

Morning Entry

Personal Note from Angel
Good morning, beautiful soul. I know life isn't always easy, and sometimes we go through difficult moments that feel overwhelming. But remember, you are never alone in your struggles. God sees you and is walking with you, even in the hardest times. Trust that He has a plan for you, even when you can't see it yet. Today, let's choose to trust Him with all of our hearts, knowing that His love will always carry us through.

Scripture (New Testament)
"Cast all your anxiety on Him because He cares for you." – 1 Peter 5:7

Poem
When the world feels heavy, and the skies are gray,
And every step forward feels miles away,
Trust in the One who sees the whole of your heart,
He's been with you since the very start.
When darkness surrounds, and your strength is gone,
Know He's beside you, holding you on.
For in your weakness, His power is shown,
He'll carry you through, so you're never alone.
He is your refuge, your guide, and your peace,
His love never falters, His grace will not cease.
So cast your cares on Him, and you will see,
In your surrender, you'll find your victory.

Reflection Questions (Morning)

1. How have you experienced God's presence during challenging times in your life?

2. What are some specific fears or worries you feel comfortable surrendering to God today?

Devotional Thought
When we are in hard times, it's easy to let fear and anxiety take over. But this scripture reminds us that God is always there to carry our burdens. He asks us to cast our worries on Him because He loves us and cares for our well-being. When we trust in His plans, even in the most difficult situations, we begin to experience peace that only He can provide. Today, take a moment to release your anxieties to God and trust that He is in control.

Prayer
Dear God,
I bring my worries and burdens before You today. I trust that You are with me, even in the hard moments. Please give me the strength to trust Your plan, even when I don't understand it. Help me feel Your peace and Your presence in every step I take. I know You care for me, and I surrender all my fears to You. .

Journaling Prompt
Take a moment to write down any fears or anxieties you are holding onto. Then, write a prayer surrendering them to God. Let this be a reminder that you are not carrying these burdens alone—God is right there with you.

Evening Entry

Personal Note from Angel
As you wind down from today, I want you to remember how loved and cherished you are. Even in the struggles you face, God is holding you close. Let His love bring you peace tonight, knowing that tomorrow is a new day to trust Him more deeply. Rest well, and let His presence fill you with hope and strength for the journey ahead.

Scripture (Old Testament)
"The Lord will fight for you; you need only to be still." – Exodus 14:14

Guided Poem

(Finish in your own words)
When the world is too much and you cannot stand,
And your heart feels burdened by a heavy hand,
Remember, dear one, that God will fight,
In His strength, you'll find your might.
He asks you to rest, to be still in His care,
For He's working behind the scenes, everywhere.
So let your soul rest, and let your heart know,
In the waiting, His love will continue to grow.
You don't have to worry, you don't have to strive,
In God's arms, you'll always thrive.

Reflection Questions (Evening)

1. How did you experience God's peace and presence in the hard moments of today?

2. How can you share God's peace and trust with someone else in your life who is struggling?

Devotional Thought
Exodus 14:14 reminds us that God is always fighting for us. We are not meant to carry the weight of the world on our shoulders. Instead, God asks us to trust Him and allow Him to work in our lives. When we take a moment to be still, we make space for God's peace to fill us. Tonight, as you reflect, remember that God is already at work, and you can trust Him to guide you through the difficulties ahead.

Prayer
Lord,
Thank You for being my constant source of strength and peace. Tonight, I rest in Your arms, trusting that You are working on my behalf. Help me to trust in Your timing and to be still in Your love. Thank You for fighting for me, even when I cannot see it. I place my worries in Your hands, and I choose to trust You.

Journaling Prompt
Take a few moments to reflect on the peace God has given you today. Write down any ways you can share His peace with someone else who may need it. How can you be an encouragement to others who are struggling?

Day 12: He Knows Your Heart

Morning Entry

Personal Note from Angel
Good morning, beautiful soul! I want to know that God sees you, not just the things you do, but who you are deep in your heart. It's easy to get caught up in the world's expectations, but remember, God knows you better than anyone else. Today, I encourage you to be still and let Him remind you that you are loved just as you are. Let His peace settle in your heart, knowing you are never alone in this journey.

Scripture (New Testament)
Matthew 6:8 – "Do not be like them, for your Father knows what you need before you ask Him."

Poem
He knows your heart, every whisper, every sigh,
The silent prayers you think only the stars can hear,
In your struggles, in your joy, He draws near,
A love that never fades, always drawing nigh.

Through quiet moments and loud, bustling days,
He walks beside you, His love never astray,
The secrets you hold, the dreams you keep,
He knows them all, even when you sleep.

Trust in His knowing, rest in His embrace,
His love is unconditional, full of grace.
No mask, no façade, no need to pretend,
He knows your heart, and He's here till the end.

Reflection Questions (Morning)

1. How does it make you feel to know that God already knows your heart and all your needs?

2. What are some areas in your life where you need to trust God more deeply?

Devotional Thought
We often feel the need to ask God for everything, but He already knows our hearts. He understands our desires, our fears, and our weaknesses even before we speak them aloud. This doesn't mean we shouldn't ask; rather, it's a reminder that He loves us so deeply and knows what's best for us. Today, rest in the truth that God sees you completely, and His love for you is unwavering. Trust in His plan and His perfect timing.

Prayer
Dear Heavenly Father,
Thank You for knowing me inside and out, for loving me despite my flaws. I pray that today, I would trust Your plans more deeply and let go of any fear that holds me back. Help me rest in Your love, knowing that You are always with me, understanding my heart. Thank You for never leaving me.
In Jesus' name,

Journaling Prompt
Take a moment to reflect on your heart—what is on your mind today? Write about the things you want to share with God, even the unspoken thoughts, and trust that He knows them already. Consider how you can surrender more to His plan today.

Evening Entry

Personal Note from Angel
As you wind down today, take a deep breath and remember that God is with you in every moment. He knows your heart and loves you beyond measure, no matter where you've been or what you've faced today. Let His peace surround you and remind you that you are held in His care. Rest in His love, and know that He is always working for your good.

Scripture (Old Testament)
Psalm 139:1-2 – "O Lord, You have searched me and known me. You know when I sit down and when I rise up; You discern my thoughts from afar."

Guided Poem

(Finish in your own words)
In the stillness, He knows your heart,
Every thought, every part.
Even when the world feels far,
He's right there, where you are.

The struggles you carry, the joys you share,
He sees them all, with loving care.
He knows your heart, your deepest plea—
How do you want to respond to His love and see?

Reflection Questions (Evening)

1. How did you experience God's presence in your day?

2. In what ways can you share God's love with someone else tomorrow?

Devotional Thought
God has searched us and knows us more deeply than we could ever imagine. He is with us in every moment, and His love never falters. As we look at our day, let us reflect on how we've experienced His knowing presence. Trust that He is guiding us even when we don't fully understand. Tomorrow, look for ways to reflect His love to others, knowing that He is working in and through you.

Prayer
Father God,
Thank You for knowing me so completely. I am in awe of Your love and care for me. Help me to trust You more and to share Your love with those around me. May my heart reflect Your grace in all I do. I trust in Your plan for me, knowing that You are always with me.
In Jesus' name,

Journaling Prompt
Think about the moments today when you felt God's love. How can you share that love with others? Write a prayer or a letter to God, expressing your gratitude and desire to reflect His love to those around you.

Day 13: Leaning on God in Prayer

Morning Entry

Personal Note from Angel
Good morning, beautiful soul! Today's focus is on prayer—how we can lean on God in those quiet, intimate moments. I've always found comfort in knowing I don't have to have the perfect words when I pray; it's the heart behind the prayer that counts. Whether you're celebrating a victory or struggling with something heavy, know that God is right there, ready to listen. Don't hesitate to pour your heart out. I pray that today, you feel His closeness in every word you speak.

Scripture (New Testament)
"Do not be anxious about anything, but in everything, by prayer and petition, with thanksgiving, present your requests to God." – Philippians 4:6

Poem
In the quiet of the morning, I bow my head,
Grateful for the peace that You have spread.
Each word I speak, though soft and low,
Is heard by You, who loves me so.

When doubt and fear weigh on my heart,
I know that from You, I'll never depart.
In prayer, I find my refuge and strength,
Leaning on You, I go the length.

My soul, it rests in Your embrace,
Each prayer a step to find Your grace.
I trust in You with all my might,
You hold me close through day and night.

Reflection Questions (Morning)

1. How do you feel when you bring your worries to God in prayer?

2. What is one prayer request you've been holding on to, trusting that God will answer in His perfect timing?

Devotional Thought
Prayer is not just about asking God for things; it's about building a relationship with Him. Philippians 4:6 reminds us to present everything to God in prayer, with thanksgiving. He wants us to share our joys, our struggles, and our dreams. When we pray, we lean into His love and grace, allowing Him to carry our burdens and bring us peace. Trust that He is listening, and know that He cares about the deepest parts of your heart.

Prayer
Lord, thank You for always being there to hear my prayers. I bring all my worries, hopes, and dreams before You today, trusting that You are working in my life. Help me to lean on You more and more, especially when I feel anxious or uncertain. I know You love me and are always with me, guiding my steps. Please give me peace as I trust in Your plan.

Journaling Prompt
Take a moment to write a prayer to God. What's been weighing on your heart lately? Pour it out to Him. Don't worry about the perfect words—just speak from your heart and trust that He is listening.

Evening Entry

Personal Note from Angel
As the day winds down, I hope you feel a sense of peace in knowing you're not alone in this journey. Prayer isn't just for the big moments—it's for every moment. I encourage you to take a few quiet minutes before you fall asleep, reflecting on the ways God has been with you today. I'm praying for you, that tonight you feel wrapped in His love.

Scripture (Old Testament)
"The Lord is near to all who call on Him, to all who call on Him in truth." – Psalm 145:18

Guided Poem

(Finish in your own words)
When I call to You, You hear my cry,
Your presence near, You're always nigh.
In my moments of doubt and fear,
You're there to hold me, drawing near.
You guide me with Your gentle hand,
Leading me to understand.

Your love surrounds me, soft and true,
And I am never far from You.

Reflection Questions (Evening)

1. How did you feel God's presence today, whether in moments of peace or struggle?

2. How can you share His love with someone else before the end of this week?

Devotional Thought
Psalm 145:18 reminds us that God is always near, ready to hear our call. No matter how small or big our prayers may be, He listens. Tonight, rest knowing that He is with you, close to your heart. When you call on Him in truth, He will answer with love and peace. You don't have to be perfect in your prayers—just honest and open, trusting that He will meet you where you are.

Prayer
Dear Lord, thank You for being near to me today. As I reflect on all that You've done in my life, I am filled with gratitude. Please help me to continue leaning on You in prayer and trust that You are guiding me each step of the way. I lay my heart before You tonight and ask for Your peace.

Journaling Prompt
As you end your day, think about the prayers God has answered, big and small. Write about the ways He has been present in your life today. Consider how you can trust Him more deeply in the days ahead.

Day 14: Embracing God's Timing

Morning Entry

Personal Note from Angel:
Good morning, beautiful soul! Today, let's focus on the importance of God's perfect timing. I know it can be hard to wait for answers or to see the bigger picture, but trust me—His timing is always better than our own. I've had moments where I felt like I was waiting forever, but in hindsight, I can see how God worked everything out just as He planned. Let's remember that every moment is part of a greater purpose, and we are never waiting in vain. Let's embrace today knowing that God's timing is always right.

Scripture (New Testament):
"But the one who endures to the end will be saved." —Matthew 24:13 (NIV)

Poem:
In every step, there's a waiting phase,
A season of growth,.in God's own ways.
Though the path may seem long and unclear,
His timing is perfect, always near.

When your heart feels heavy, and hope is thin,
Know that God's work is deep within.
Every delay holds a gift unknown,
A blessing designed for you alone.

Trust in the rhythm, the ebb and flow,
God's timing will lead you where you need to go.
His plan is unfolding, so let it unfold,
For the story He writes is better than told.

Reflection Questions (Morning):

1. How do you feel when you think about waiting on God's timing in your life?

2. Can you think of a moment when God's timing surprised you and worked out better than you expected?

Devotional Thought:
God's timing can be a challenge to trust, especially when we are anxious or unsure of what comes next. But He promises that those who endure will be rewarded. Every season of waiting is an opportunity for us to grow in faith and patience. While we may not understand why we must wait, we can trust that God has a plan that will work out for our good. The key is in learning to embrace His timing and resting in the assurance that He's got everything under control.

Prayer:
Lord, thank You for Your perfect timing. I confess that sometimes it's hard to wait, but I trust that You have a plan for me. Help me to embrace each moment and grow in patience. Teach me to trust in Your timing, knowing that You are always working behind the scenes for my good. Thank You for being faithful and for leading me exactly where I need to be. .

Journaling Prompt:
Take a moment to think about a time when waiting on God's timing brought you peace. Write about how you felt during that wait and how you saw God's hand in your life through that season. What did you learn during the wait?

Evening Entry

Personal Note from Angel:
As the day comes to a close, I hope you are reminded of how much trust God places in you. He knows you are capable of waiting, growing, and enduring. Reflecting on His timing today can bring peace into our hearts as we rest. There's comfort in knowing that we are never alone in our waiting. Remember, God's timing is a gift, and He will never leave us to wait without purpose.

Scripture (Old Testament):
"For everything there is a season, and a time for every matter under heaven." —Ecclesiastes 3:1 (ESV)

Guided Poem:

(Finish in your own words)
The waiting is hard, but I know He's near,
In every delay, I sense His care.
When the road is long, and the night is cold,
I trust His timing, so I'm not afraid to be bold.

He leads me through seasons of change and growth,
Reminding me always to trust in His oath.
For every moment, there's a plan designed,
And I wait for His timing, knowing I'm aligned.

Reflection Questions (Evening):

1. How did you experience God's timing today, even in small ways?

2. Have you had a chance to share the peace of trusting in God's timing with someone else today? How can you encourage others in this way?

Devotional Thought:
God's timing is not only about waiting, it's about trusting Him through the process. In the Old Testament, Ecclesiastes reminds us that there is a time for everything under heaven, and that includes the moments when we feel like we are waiting. Tonight, as we reflect on this, let's focus on the peace that comes from trusting that God is in control. Our wait is never wasted; He is working all things together for our good, even when we can't see the full picture.

Prayer:
Father, thank You for always being right on time. I rest in the knowledge that You have every moment of my life in Your hands. Help me to trust Your timing more deeply and to share this trust with others. As I end this day, I pray for peace and patience in the days to come.

Journaling Prompt:
Think about someone in your life who may be struggling with trusting God's timing. Write them a letter of encouragement, sharing the peace and hope you have found in knowing that God's timing is always perfect. What would you want to remind them of tonight?

Day 15: The Strength in Your Weakness

Morning Entry

Personal Note from Angel
Good morning, beautiful soul! Sometimes we can feel overwhelmed by our weaknesses, but it's in those moments that we experience God's strength the most. I've had times where I felt completely inadequate, but God met me there, showing me that my weaknesses are simply a canvas for His power. I want you to remember that it's okay to not have everything figured out. God uses our imperfections for His glory. Lean into Him today—He is your strength.

Scripture (New Testament)
2 Corinthians 12:9 – "But he said to me, 'My grace is sufficient for you, for my power is made perfect in weakness.' Therefore I will boast all the more gladly of my weaknesses, so that the power of Christ may rest upon me."

Poem
In moments of doubt, when strength seems small,
God whispers softly, "You are not alone at all."
The weight of the world can press you low,
But in your weakness, His power will grow.
Each broken part becomes a place of grace,
As He fills the void and shows His face.
In the storm, you may feel lost,
But God's strength will cover every cost.
So when you fall, rise once more,
For His love will open every door.
Your weakness will become His light,
Shining through the dark of night.

Reflection Questions (Morning)

1. How do you feel about your own weaknesses today? Are you able to see them as an opportunity for God to show His strength?

2. Can you think of a time when God's power was evident in your weakness? What did that teach you about His love and grace?

Devotional Thought
Sometimes, we think we have to be strong on our own to be worthy of God's love and purpose. But the truth is, it's when we are weakest that we allow His strength to shine. God's grace is more than enough to carry us through. When we stop trying to fix everything ourselves and lean into Him, we allow His power to rest on us. His strength is perfect in our weakness, and He loves us through it all.

Prayer
Lord, I feel weak today, but I trust that Your strength is made perfect in my weakness. Help me embrace my limitations and lean on You for the strength I need. I know that You will never leave me or forsake me, and in that, I find peace. Please fill me with Your grace and power today. .

Journaling Prompt
Take a moment to reflect on a time when you felt weak but experienced God's strength in a powerful way. Write about how that moment impacted your faith and what you learned about trusting God in your weaknesses.

Evening Entry

Personal Note from Angel
As you reflect on your day, I want to remind you that you are exactly where you need to be. Even in your moments of weakness, God is at work, making you stronger than you can imagine. Trust that He has been with you every step of the way. Take a deep breath and know that His grace is sufficient, and tomorrow is a new day to lean into His strength. Rest well, knowing He is with you always.

Scripture (Old Testament)
Isaiah 40:29 – "He gives power to the faint, and to him who has no might he increases strength."

Guided Poem

(Finish in your own words)
When I feel faint, I call Your name,
And You give me strength, You take the blame.
In my weakness, I see Your grace,
You fill the gap, You take my place.
Though I stumble, You hold me fast,
Your love makes me strong, and it will last.
The weight of the world cannot take me down,
For You lift me up, You wear the crown.
..

Reflection Questions (Evening)

1. How did you experience God's strength in your weakness today?

2. How can you share the encouragement of God's strength with someone else tomorrow?

Devotional Thought
Throughout the day, we may encounter moments where we feel tired, discouraged, or overwhelmed. But in those times, remember God's promise to give us strength when we are faint. His grace will always be enough to carry us through. When we recognize our weakness, we make room for His power to work in us. Trust that He is always there to help, even when we feel incapable.

Prayer
Father, thank You for the strength You give when I am weak. I am grateful for Your presence in my life, and I trust that You will always be my source of strength. Help me rest in You tonight, knowing that You will carry me through tomorrow.

Journaling Prompt
Take a moment to write about how God gave you strength today. Reflect on any weaknesses you noticed in yourself and how you saw God working through them. Write a letter to God expressing your gratitude for His strength and grace.

Day 16: Walking by Faith, Not Sight

Morning Entry

Personal Note from Angel
Good morning, beautiful soul! Sometimes it feels like we're walking through the fog, not able to see what lies ahead. But remember, God asks us to walk by faith, not by sight. Trust that He's guiding each step, even when the path is unclear. I know it can be hard, but when you choose faith over fear, you'll see His plan unfold in ways you never imagined. Today, let's remember that even in uncertainty, God is sure. I'm praying for you as you take each step in trust.

Scripture (New Testament)
For we walk by faith, not by sight.
—2 Corinthians 5:7

Poem
Though the way is shrouded in night,
I walk by faith, trusting His light.
Each step uncertain, yet I trust,
That He will guide me through the dust.
When I can't see what lies ahead,
I know He'll lead me, where He's led.
His hand is steady, His heart is true,
And in my doubt, His love breaks through.
I don't need to know the way,
For He is with me every day.
I walk by faith, not what I see,
For He is all I need to be.

Reflection Questions (Morning)

1. How do you feel when you don't know what's ahead? How can you surrender your worries to God today?

2. What are some moments where you've seen God's faithfulness, even when you couldn't see His plan clearly?

Devotional Thought
Walking by faith doesn't mean we have all the answers; it's trusting God even when we can't see the full picture. There's beauty in stepping forward with Him, knowing that each step is a part of His greater plan. God doesn't promise a smooth journey, but He promises to be with us through every moment. Faith is about trusting that He's already walked the path before us and will guide us through every twist and turn. Embrace the unknown today, knowing He holds you in His hands.

Prayer
Lord, I confess that sometimes I want to know the whole plan, but I know You're asking me to walk by faith. Please help me trust You in moments of doubt. Remind me that You are always with me, guiding my steps even when I can't see the way. Fill my heart with peace as I choose to trust Your plan. Thank You for Your unwavering love.

Journaling Prompt
Reflect on a time when you had to step out in faith. How did it feel in the moment? What did you learn from it? Write a prayer asking God to help you trust Him more fully in your current circumstances.

Evening Entry

Personal Note from Angel
As the day winds down, I hope you've felt His presence with you every step of the way. Remember, walking by faith isn't a one-time decision—it's a daily choice. Today, I encourage you to rest in the peace that comes from knowing God is in control. You don't have to have everything figured out. Just rest in His love tonight, knowing that He's holding you through every uncertainty.

Scripture (Old Testament)
The Lord will fight for you; you need only to be still.
—Exodus 14:14

Guided Poem

(Finish in your own words)
In the quiet of the night,
I find my rest, though out of sight.
You've walked with me through every test,
And in Your love, I find my rest.
The battle's not for me to fight,
For You, O Lord, are my delight.
In stillness, I can hear Your voice,
You lead me, God, I will rejoice.
And when the way is unclear,
I trust You are always near.

Reflection Questions (Evening)

1. How did you trust God today, even when you couldn't see what was ahead?

2. Who can you reach out to and share God's peace with tonight? How can you be a reminder of His faithfulness to others?

Devotional Thought
Exodus 14:14 reminds us that sometimes the best thing we can do is simply be still and let God fight for us. We don't have to have all the answers or control the outcome. Faith means trusting God to handle what we cannot. As we walk by faith, we also learn to rest in Him, trusting that He's got it all under control.

Prayer
God, thank You for fighting for me today. I rest in Your love tonight, knowing that I don't have to figure it all out. I choose to trust You with my tomorrow, knowing You are already there. Help me to be still and find peace in Your presence.

Journaling Prompt
Take a moment to reflect on how God has been faithful in your life. Write down any worries you need to hand over to Him tonight and trust that He's already at work.

Day 17: Understanding God's Purpose for You

Morning Entry

Personal Note from Angel

Hey there, beautiful! I know sometimes it can feel hard to understand what God's purpose for your life really is. It might seem like you're walking through a fog, unsure of which path to take. But here's the thing—God has already paved the way for you. Trust in His timing, and remember that even when we don't have all the answers, He is working everything out for good. I'm with you on this journey, and we'll discover more of His plan for us together, one step at a time.

Scripture (New Testament)

"For I know the plans I have for you," declares the Lord, "plans to prosper you and not to harm you, plans to give you a hope and a future." — Jeremiah 29:11

Poem

God's plan, though unseen,
Is a map written in stars.
Every twist and turn,
Every stumble, every scar.
His love surrounds you,
A light in the dark,
Guiding your steps,
Leaving His mark.
Trust, dear heart,
Even when you can't see,
His purpose for you
Is as certain as the sea.
Hold on to His promises,
Through every tear and sigh,
For God's plan is perfect—
And it will never pass by.

Reflection Questions (Morning)

1. How do you feel about the idea that God has a plan for your life?

2. What are some of the ways you've seen God's purpose unfold in your life so far?

Devotional Thought
Understanding God's purpose for you doesn't always happen overnight. Sometimes, it's revealed little by little as we take each step in faith. But one thing is certain—God's plans are always for your good. Even in moments when things seem unclear, trust that He is working things together for His greater purpose. Keep your heart open to His guidance and His voice, and you'll begin to see how He is shaping you for something beautiful.

Prayer
Dear God,
I trust that You have a perfect plan for my life, even when I can't see the full picture. Help me to trust in Your timing and to rest in Your love. Guide me today, Lord, as I seek to understand more of the purpose You have for me. Thank You for never leaving me alone in this journey.

Journaling Prompt
Reflect on a time when you felt God guiding you in a specific way. Write about the experience and how it made you feel closer to His purpose for your life. How can you trust Him more fully today?

Evening Entry

Personal Note from Angel
As you unwind tonight, remember that the journey of discovering God's purpose for you is ongoing. It's okay if things aren't clear right now—take comfort in knowing that you are right where He wants you to be. God's plan is always unfolding, and with each day, you grow closer to understanding it. Take a deep breath, rest in His love, and trust that tomorrow will bring new insights.

Scripture (Old Testament)
"The Lord will fulfill His purpose for me; your love, O Lord, endures forever—do not abandon the works of Your hands." — Psalm 138:8

Guided Poem

(Finish in your own words)
God's purpose for me,
So deep, so wide,
I trust in Your love,
And the paths You provide.
I know I am here,
For a reason, a call,
Even when I'm unsure,
I trust in it all.
I walk by Your side,
Through storm and through strife—
Lord, help me to see,

Reflection Questions (Evening)

1. How have you seen God's love in action today?

2. How can you share God's purpose for your life with someone else tomorrow?

Devotional Thought
As we reflect on the day, let's remember that God's purpose for us is not just about where we go or what we do. It's about who we are becoming in Him. We are His workmanship, and He is always at work in us. Trust that His plan is unfolding, and know that He will continue to guide you, day by day, toward His greater purpose.

Prayer
Dear Heavenly Father,
Thank You for Your unfailing love and for the purpose You've placed on my life. Help me to rest in Your plans and to trust in Your timing. Tonight, I surrender my worries and my uncertainties to You. I trust that You are fulfilling Your purpose in me, and I am excited for the path ahead.

Journaling Prompt
Write about a recent moment when you felt God's purpose in your life. How did it impact you? What steps can you take tomorrow to trust God more fully in your journey?

Day 18: Finding Peace in Surrender

Morning Entry

Personal Note from Angel:
Good morning, beautiful soul! I know sometimes it feels like we're carrying a lot, and it can be hard to let go. But today, I want you to know that finding peace comes from surrendering it all to God. It's not about having all the answers or being in control, but trusting that He has a perfect plan for you. Take a deep breath, and let this day be about finding rest in His arms. You are loved, just as you are. God is with you, always.

Scripture (New Testament):
"Come to me, all you who are weary and burdened, and I will give you rest." —Matthew 11:28

Poem:
In the quiet moments, we come undone,
Tired from the journey, seeking the Son.
The weight we carry, too much to bear,
But in His presence, He's always there.

Surrendering hearts, letting go of fear,
God's gentle whisper, "I am near."
Rest in His arms, let the struggle cease,
In surrender, we find perfect peace.

When the world feels heavy and our souls are tired,
God's love wraps us up, and we're inspired.
Trust in His plan, it's all we need,
In surrender, we are set free.

Reflection Questions (Morning):

1. *How do you feel about surrendering control to God today?*

2. *What is one area of your life where you can trust Him more fully?*

Devotional Thought:
God invites us to come to Him with our burdens, offering peace and rest. When we surrender, we release the weight that we were never meant to carry alone. Finding peace in surrender is not about giving up, but about trusting that His plan is greater than our own. In letting go, we make space for God's grace to fill us up and guide us. This peace doesn't depend on our circumstances—it's found in our trust in Him.

Prayer:
Lord, I come to You with a heart that longs for peace. Help me release my burdens and trust You more fully. Thank You for being a safe place to surrender my worries and fears. I ask for Your strength and guidance as I walk with You today.

Journaling Prompt:
Take a moment to write about an area in your life where you're struggling to let go. What would it look like to surrender it to God today? How can you find peace in trusting Him more fully?

Evening Entry

Personal Note from Angel:
As you wind down tonight, I hope you feel a sense of peace that comes with surrender. God knows our hearts and desires for us to find rest in Him. There's no need to carry the weight alone, and tonight, I pray you feel the freedom of letting go. Reflect on His goodness and how He has carried you today. Sleep well, knowing He holds you in His hands.

Scripture (Old Testament):
"The Lord will fight for you; you need only to be still." —Exodus 14:14

Guided Poem:

(Finish in your own words)
At the end of the day, we rest our minds,
Trusting God's plan, leaving worries behind.
The battle is His, the victory too,
And in His love, we are made new.

He calls us to be still, to wait in grace,
To trust in His timing, in His embrace.
In moments of peace, our souls find rest,
Knowing we're held in the arms of the Blessed.

Reflection Questions (Evening):

1. How did you see God's love in your life today?

2. In what ways can you share this peace and love with someone else tomorrow?

Devotional Thought:
Tonight, we reflect on the truth that God fights for us. Our battles aren't ours to fight alone—He is with us, every step of the way. As we surrender, He takes the weight, and we experience peace. Being still allows us to trust more deeply in His presence. It's in this stillness that we find rest for our souls, knowing that He's always at work for our good.

Prayer:
Lord, thank You for Your peace and for fighting our battles. Tonight, I surrender all my worries to You, knowing You are in control. Help me to be still and trust in Your love. Fill me with Your peace, and help me share that peace with others tomorrow..

Journaling Prompt:
Write a letter to God, telling Him what you are surrendering today. Ask Him to fill you with peace and trust as you let go of your burdens. Reflect on how this surrender has brought you closer to Him.

Day 19: Trusting God with Your Future

Morning Entry

Personal Note from Angel
Good morning, beautiful soul. I know it can feel uncertain when we think about the future, and sometimes we may even wonder if we're on the right path. But I want to remind you today that God has a perfect plan for your life, even when the steps ahead seem unclear. Trusting Him with our future doesn't mean having all the answers—it means believing He's got it under control, even when we don't. You are never alone in your journey, and God is working behind the scenes on your behalf. Rest in that today, and let His peace guide your heart.

Scripture (New Testament)
"For I know the plans I have for you, declares the Lord, plans for welfare and not for evil, to give you a future and a hope." – Jeremiah 29:11

Poem
The future unfolds like a mystery,
Hidden in grace, yet plain to see.
God's hand is guiding every way,
With love that leads us through each day.

Though we may stumble, though we may fear,
His promises draw ever near.
In every twist, in every turn,
His steady love, we'll always learn.

Rest in His promise, and you will see,
That your future's safe, so trust in Me.

Reflection Questions (Morning)

1. How does it feel to know that God has a plan for your life, even when the future seems uncertain?

2. What steps can you take today to trust God more with your future?

Devotional Thought
Today, we're reminded that God has a purpose for our lives—an incredible future filled with His hope and peace. Sometimes, we want to control every detail, but true trust comes when we release our fears and surrender our future into His hands. His plan is far better than any we could dream up, and His love will see us through the twists and turns. Let's take comfort in knowing that we don't have to know it all; we just have to trust the One who does.

Prayer
Dear God,
I lay my future in Your hands today. I trust that You have a plan for me, a plan filled with hope and purpose. Help me to release my worries and follow Your guidance with a heart full of faith. I know that no matter what comes, You are with me, and You will lead me through. Thank You for Your love and grace.

Journaling Prompt
Take a moment to reflect on any fears or uncertainties you have about the future. Write a prayer or a statement of trust, surrendering those worries to God. Ask Him to help you see His plan clearly and to give you peace as you walk forward.

Evening Entry

Personal Note from Angel
As you end your day, I want you to rest in the peace that comes from knowing God is in control. You don't have to have everything figured out, and that's okay. Trust is a journey, and you are walking it with Him by your side. Let your heart be filled with gratitude for the steps you've taken today, and know that God is leading you toward a beautiful future. I'm so proud of you for trusting Him.

Scripture (Old Testament)
"Trust in the Lord with all your heart, and lean not on your own understanding. In all your ways acknowledge Him, and He will make straight your paths." – Proverbs 3:5-6

Guided Poem

(Finish in your own words)
Trusting God with all I am,
I place my life within His hand.
Though I can't see what lies ahead,
I know His love will lead instead.

My future's bright, my hope is sure,
For in His plan, I am secure.

Reflection Questions (Evening)

1. How did you experience God's peace and trust today?

2. How can you share your trust in God's plan with others, encouraging them to trust Him too?

Devotional Thought
As we end the day, let's reflect on the ways God has been faithful to us. We may not have all the answers, but we can trust that He is guiding us every step of the way. Let's lean not on our own understanding but on His perfect plan, knowing that He will make our paths straight. Our future is secure in His hands, and that truth brings peace to our hearts.

Prayer
God,
Thank You for today. I trust that You are guiding me and leading me toward the future You've planned for me. Help me to continue trusting You, especially when I don't understand what's ahead. Fill my heart with peace, knowing that You hold my future in Your hands. Thank You for Your never-ending love and faithfulness.

Journaling Prompt
Reflect on any moments today where you saw God working in your life or felt His peace. Write down a prayer of gratitude, thanking Him for His guidance and trustworthiness. Consider how you can share this peace with others, letting them see the hope and trust you have in God's plan.

Day 20: God's Plan is Greater Than Our Own

Morning Entry

Personal Note from Angel
Good morning, beautiful! Sometimes, it's hard to trust that God has a plan when things don't seem to go the way we expect. But remember, His plan is always better than anything we could imagine. I've learned that when I'm unsure, it's okay to lean into Him, trusting that His timing is perfect. Take a deep breath and remember, even when things seem out of our control, God is always at work behind the scenes. You are never alone in this journey.

Scripture (New Testament)
"For I know the plans I have for you, declares the Lord, plans for welfare and not for evil, to give you a future and a hope."
— Jeremiah 29:11 (ESV)

Poem
God's plans are not our own,
They're greater than we've ever known.
In moments of doubt, we must trust,
That His way is always just.
We might not see, but we can know,
He's guiding us where we need to go.
Through every struggle, every fight,
He leads us gently toward the light.
His timing perfect, His love so deep,
In Him, our hearts and souls will keep.
Trust the journey, He's by your side,
For in His plan, you will reside.

Reflection Questions (Morning)

1. How does it feel knowing that God has a specific plan for your life, even when you don't fully understand it?

2. What is one area of your life where you can trust God more deeply, surrendering control to His plan?

Devotional Thought
Sometimes we think we know what's best for us, but God's plan surpasses our own. His vision for our lives is rooted in His deep love for us and His understanding of what's best for our growth. It's not always easy to surrender, but when we lean into God's will, we're saying, "I trust you." Trusting God means believing that His plan, though it may look different from what we envisioned, is filled with hope, purpose, and good things for our future.

Prayer
Dear God,
Thank you for the reminder that Your plan for me is greater than anything I could create on my own. Help me trust You more today and embrace the path You have laid out for me. I know Your ways are higher, and I want to lean into Your wisdom and grace. Please guide me in moments of doubt, and help me see the beauty of Your plan unfolding in my life.

Journaling Prompt
Reflect on the areas of your life where you're holding onto your own plans. How can you release these to God today? Write a prayer surrendering those parts of your life to His perfect plan.

Evening Entry

Personal Note from Angel
As your day winds down, I want to remind you that God's plan is always in motion, even when we can't see it. Trust that everything is happening for your good, even the hard moments. Take time tonight to be grateful for the steps He's already taken with you, and know that tomorrow, His plan continues. I'm praying for you as you rest, that you'll sleep in peace knowing that God is in control.

Scripture (Old Testament)
"The heart of man plans his way, but the Lord establishes his steps."
— Proverbs 16:9 (ESV)

Guided Poem

(Finish in your own words)
I plan my way, I make my move,
But God directs where I will prove.
His steps are steady, His path is clear,
I trust His guidance, without fear.
Though my own plans may change today,
I trust His will in every way.
His wisdom greater, His love so deep,
In Him, my soul finds peace to keep.

Reflection Questions (Evening)

1. How did you see God's plan unfold in your life today, even in small ways?

2. In what ways can you share the trust you have in God's plan with someone else?

Devotional Thought
As we go about our lives, we may have our own plans, but ultimately, it's God who establishes our steps. The beauty is in trusting Him, knowing that His way is always the right way. When we focus on His love and faithfulness, we can rest assured that we are walking exactly where He wants us to be. Trusting in His plan doesn't mean there won't be struggles, but it does mean He will never leave us, and He will always guide us.

Prayer
Lord,
I thank You for the guidance You provide in my life. Help me trust in Your plans more fully and accept Your direction, even when I can't see where it's taking me. May Your peace surround me tonight as I rest in Your loving care, knowing that I am right where You want me to be.

Journaling Prompt
Take a moment to reflect on the steps you took today. How did you see God's presence guiding your actions, even in moments of uncertainty? Write about it and express gratitude for His faithfulness.

Day 21: Living in His Grace

Morning Entry

Personal Note from Angel
Good morning, beautiful! As we step into this new day, I want you to remember that God's grace is all around you. It's easy to feel like we need to be perfect, but His grace is perfect, and it's given freely. Today, take a moment to reflect on His grace in your life, whether it's in the little blessings or the big moments. His love is constant, and no matter what you face, His grace will always be enough. You are never alone, and His arms are always open to you.

Scripture (New Testament)
"But he said to me, 'My grace is sufficient for you, for my power is made perfect in weakness.' Therefore I will boast all the more gladly of my weaknesses, so that the power of Christ may rest upon me." — 2 Corinthians 12:9

Poem
In the quiet of your heart,
Grace whispers softly, plays its part,
A gentle touch, a soothing balm,
Bringing peace, a steady calm.
Through every storm and restless night,
God's grace will always be your light.
In moments when you feel unsure,
His love and mercy will endure.
His grace, a gift that never ends,
A faithful presence, your true friend.
So rest in Him, and know it's true,
His grace is always there for you.

Reflection Questions (Morning)

1. How does God's grace show up in your life today?

2. When you feel weak or overwhelmed, how can you remind yourself that God's grace is enough?

Devotional Thought
Grace isn't just a word; it's the living presence of God in our lives. We often see our weaknesses as hindrances, but God sees them as opportunities for His power to shine through. When we feel like we're not enough, grace steps in and makes us whole. Embrace your weaknesses and trust that God's grace is doing a mighty work in you. Every day, every moment, His grace is sufficient.

Prayer
Dear God, thank You for Your amazing grace. Help me to see Your grace in my life today, especially in my weaknesses. I trust that You are working in me, and I surrender my struggles to You. Fill me with Your strength and remind me that Your grace is always enough. Amen.

Journaling Prompt
Take a moment to reflect on the areas of your life where you need God's grace today. Write down your thoughts and offer them to God in prayer, trusting that He will carry you through.

Evening Entry

Personal Note from Angel
As the day winds down, I want you to know how proud I am of you. You've made it through another day, and I pray that you've felt God's grace surrounding you. Remember, even in the hardest moments, His grace is still with you. As you rest tonight, let go of the weight of the day and trust that His love will carry you through tomorrow. Sleep peacefully knowing that God's grace covers you.

Scripture (Old Testament)
"But the Lord God is a sun and shield; the Lord bestows favor and honor. No good thing does he withhold from those who walk uprightly." — Psalm 84:11

Guided Poem

(Finish in your own words)
God's grace is like the sun above,
Shining down with endless love.
In each moment, He's here with me,
His love and mercy setting me free.
When darkness falls, I trust His light,
Guiding me through the darkest night.
His favor is a shield around,
A love that's sure, a love that's found.

Reflection Questions (Evening)

1. How did you feel God's love and grace today?

2. How can you share His grace with someone else tomorrow?

Devotional Thought
God's grace isn't something we earn—it's freely given. When we walk with Him, He blesses us with favor and honors our trust in Him. Tonight, reflect on His goodness and remember that He is with you every step of the way. No good thing will He withhold from those who trust in His love.

Prayer
Thank You, God, for Your grace that shines like the sun. Thank You for Your favor and the blessings You've poured into my life today. I trust in Your protection and love. Help me to share Your grace with others tomorrow.

Journaling Prompt
Tonight, recount some of the blessings you've experienced today. What were moments where you felt God's grace, even in the small things? Write a letter to God expressing your gratitude for His faithfulness.

Day 22: Unconditionally Loved by God

Morning Entry

Personal Note from Angel:

Good morning, sweet friend. Today, I want you to know that no matter what you may be feeling, God's love for you is unshakable. His love isn't based on anything you do or don't do; it's simply there, always available, and completely unconditional. I've struggled to grasp this truth sometimes, especially when I feel unworthy, but the beautiful thing is that God's love is never dependent on our perfection. His love is already there, just waiting for us to accept it. Today, remember that His love is constant, no matter what.

Scripture (New Testament):

"But God demonstrates His own love for us in this: While we were still sinners, Christ died for us."
— Romans 5:8

Poem:

Unseen, unheard, we wander through the day,
Seeking worth in places that only lead astray.
But here, beneath the stars, within our hearts,
God's love calls us to rest, to be whole again, apart.
No strings attached, no conditions to meet,
He loved us first, His love so sweet.
When we feel lost, alone, or small,
He's there with open arms, ready to catch us when we fall.
No need for masks, no need for pretenses,
His love is true, pure, without defenses.
Let His love wrap around your heart today,
For you are cherished in every way.

Reflection Questions (Morning):

1. How does it feel to know that God loves you unconditionally, no matter your mistakes or flaws?

2. What can you do today to remind yourself of God's unwavering love?

Devotional Thought:

God's love is not a distant or conditional love. It's not something we can earn, nor is it something we can lose. His love is a deep, unfailing commitment to us, even when we can't see or feel it. Romans 5:8 reminds us that Christ's sacrifice was made while we were still sinners, showing that God's love isn't based on our behavior. Today, let that truth settle deeply in your heart. His love is yours, and it is freely given, even in the moments when you feel unworthy.

Prayer:

Dear God,
Thank You for loving me without limits. I know that I don't deserve such a love, but You give it freely. Help me to accept Your love in a deeper way today and share that love with others. Thank You for Your grace, which never runs out. Please remind me throughout this day that Your love is constant, and I am never alone.

Journaling Prompt:

Take a moment to write down the ways in which you've experienced God's unconditional love. What are the moments when you've felt His love most strongly? How can you reflect that love to others today?

Evening Entry

Personal Note from Angel:

As the day winds down, I hope you feel peaceful and loved. God's love isn't something that fades at the end of the day. It's there in every moment, whether we are awake or resting. As you reflect on the day, remember that His love is constant, and there's nothing you can do to make Him love you more or less. Take comfort in knowing you are deeply loved and accepted by the Creator of the universe.

Scripture (Old Testament):

"The Lord appeared to us in the past, saying: 'I have loved you with an everlasting love; I have drawn you with unfailing kindness.'"
— Jeremiah 31:3

Guided Poem:

(Finish in your own words)

God's love surrounds me, steady and true,
A light that guides me, no matter what I do.
When fear or doubt tries to steal my peace,
His love remains, offering sweet release.
I don't have to earn it, I don't have to strive,
His love sustains me, keeping me alive.
It's always here, constant, and near,
A perfect love, without any fear.
I know He loves me, through every high and low,
His everlasting love will never let me go.

Reflection Questions (Evening):

1. How did you experience God's love today, even in the small moments?

2. In what ways did you share God's love with others today, or how can you plan to do so tomorrow?

Devotional Thought:

Jeremiah 31:3 reminds us that God's love is everlasting. His love is not temporary or fleeting; it's steadfast and eternal. This should bring us so much peace, especially as we reflect on our day. Even when we face challenges or feel alone, God's love is there, never changing, always consistent. Remember this truth as you rest tonight: you are deeply loved, and nothing can separate you from that love.

Prayer:

Lord,
Thank You for Your never-ending love. As I reflect on the day, I am in awe of Your kindness and grace. Please help me to rest tonight, knowing that Your love surrounds me. I want to carry that love into tomorrow and share it with those around me. Thank You for drawing me close to You, no matter where I am.

Journaling Prompt:

Reflect on the ways you have felt God's love today, and how you might share it with someone tomorrow. What is one small act of kindness you can do in His name? Write down your thoughts and ask God to help you live out His love.

Day 23: The Joy of His Presence

Morning Entry

Personal Note from Angel
Good morning, beautiful soul. Today, I want to remind you that God's presence is always with us, even when we don't feel it. There is a joy that comes from knowing that God is by our side, in every moment, in every circumstance. When we invite His presence into our lives, we open ourselves up to a peace and joy that nothing else can provide. Let this truth wash over you today as you step forward into whatever this day holds. You are never alone—He is with you, always.

Scripture (New Testament)
"In Your presence there is fullness of joy; at Your right hand are pleasures forevermore." – Psalm 16:11 (NKJV)

Poem
In the stillness, He draws near,
A whisper soft, a voice sincere.
His presence fills the room we share,
A peace that calms, beyond compare.
His love, a light that never fades,
A joy that in our hearts cascades.
No matter where we walk or run,
His presence shines like morning sun.
When darkness tries to steal our way,
He's there to guide, to light our day.
Oh, how His love ignites our hearts,
A joy that stays, no matter where we start.

Reflection Questions (Morning)

1. How do you feel God's presence in your daily life? Is there a particular moment or space where you sense Him most?

2. What are the areas in your life where you need to invite His joy more fully today?

Devotional Thought

God's presence is not just a distant idea; it's a tangible, living reality. When we seek Him, He fills our lives with His joy. This joy doesn't depend on our circumstances; it flows from His unchanging love and faithfulness. It's a joy that remains with us, even in trials. When you feel weighed down today, remember that His presence is there to lift you up. He's near, ready to offer peace and joy that only He can give.

Prayer

Father God, thank You for being with me today and every day. I invite Your presence into my heart and my life. Help me to find joy in Your nearness, no matter what comes my way. Fill me with the peace that only You can provide, and help me share that peace with those around me.

Journaling Prompt

Take a moment to reflect on the joy that comes from being in God's presence. Write about a time when you felt God near and the joy that filled your heart. How can you carry that joy with you today?

Evening Entry

Personal Note from Angel
As the day winds down, I encourage you to reflect on the joy you experienced today—whether in quiet moments, big victories, or small blessings. Remember, His presence is still with you as you rest tonight. You don't have to be active for God to be near. In the quiet, He is there, offering peace and comfort. Let His presence be the last thing you hold onto before you close your eyes tonight.

Scripture (Old Testament)
"The Lord is near to all who call upon Him, to all who call upon Him in truth." – Psalm 145:18 (NKJV)

Guided Poem

(Finish in your own words)
God, You're near when I am still,
You guide my heart, my mind, my will.
When darkness tries to steal my peace,
In Your presence, all fears cease.
I call upon You, Lord, in truth,
Knowing You will guide my youth.
With every step, with every breath,
You're near to me, through life and death.

Reflection Questions (Evening)

1. How did you experience God's presence today? Was there a moment where you felt especially close to Him?

2. How can you share the peace of God with someone else this evening or tomorrow?

Devotional Thought
As we rest tonight, let's remember that God is near, listening to every prayer, every whisper of our hearts. When we call on Him in truth, He draws near to us with love and care. This assurance helps us sleep in peace, knowing that the God of the universe is by our side, offering comfort and joy that no circumstance can steal.

Prayer
Dear God, thank You for being close to me today. As I rest tonight, may Your presence bring me peace. Thank You for Your constant love and for guiding me through each moment. I trust that You will be with me as I sleep and that You'll be near when I wake.

Journaling Prompt
Reflect on God's nearness throughout your day. Write about a specific moment where you felt His presence and how it impacted you. What does it mean to you to know that God is always near?

Day 24: Understanding Your Identity in Christ

Morning Entry

Personal Note from Angel
Good morning, beautiful! Today's message is a reminder that your true identity is found in Christ alone. When the world tries to define you by what you do, what you look like, or what others say about you, always remember that you are first and foremost His beloved daughter. You don't have to prove yourself to anyone because He already sees you as worthy and loved. My prayer for you today is that you'll embrace this truth and walk in the confidence that comes from knowing who you are in Christ.

Scripture (New Testament)
"Therefore, if anyone is in Christ, the new creation has come: The old has gone, the new is here!"
—2 Corinthians 5:17

Poem
You are more than what the world can see,
A masterpiece of grace, of love, set free.
In Christ, you've been made new, reborn,
A child of God, loved and adorned.
No longer bound by past mistakes,
A new identity your heart now takes.
The chains that once defined your soul,
Are gone, replaced by love that makes you whole.
You are His, and He is yours,
A life of peace, a love that endures.
So walk in grace, with strength and might,
For you are His child, shining bright.

Reflection Questions (Morning)

1. How do you feel about the idea of your identity being rooted in Christ?

2. Are there any areas in your life where you struggle to see yourself as God sees you?

Devotional Thought
As we reflect on today's scripture, it's so important to remember that our identity in Christ is unshakable. When we accept Him into our lives, we are made new. The old is gone—the guilt, shame, and fear no longer have a hold on us. We don't have to be defined by our past or by the labels others put on us. Instead, we can stand firm in the truth that we are beloved children of God. Embrace that new identity today, knowing that it comes with His love and grace.

Prayer
Dear God, thank You for making me a new creation in Christ. I'm so grateful for the love and grace that You have poured over me. Help me to see myself the way You see me—worthy, loved, and whole. Teach me to walk confidently in this new identity, free from the weight of my past. May I always find my worth in You alone.

Journaling Prompt
Take a moment to reflect on your identity in Christ. Write down any thoughts, feelings, or challenges you may have when it comes to fully embracing this truth. How does knowing that you are a new creation in Christ change how you see yourself today?

Evening Entry

Personal Note from Angel
Hey sweet girl, as you reflect on today, I want you to remember that your identity in Christ is not something that fades—it's something that's here to stay, no matter what challenges you face. Even on hard days, when you don't feel your best or when doubts creep in, hold fast to the truth that God sees you as His beloved. You are more than enough, just as you are. Sleep well tonight, knowing you are safe in His love.

Scripture (Old Testament)
"But now, this is what the Lord says—he who created you, Jacob, he who formed you, Israel: 'Do not fear, for I have redeemed you; I have summoned you by name; you are mine.'"
—Isaiah 43:1

Guided Poem

(Finish in your own words)
God who formed me with love so pure,
In You, my heart is safe and sure.
You know my name, and call me Yours,
Your love for me, it forever soars.
When I doubt and feel alone,
I know I'm never on my own.
You've claimed me as Your child, so dear—

Reflection Questions (Evening)

1. How did you experience God's love today?

2. In what ways did you share God's love with someone else today?

Devotional Thought
As we end our day, remember that God knows you intimately. He calls you by name because you belong to Him. There's nothing you need to do to earn His love—He simply loves you because you are His. Embrace this truth as you rest tonight. Let it give you peace, knowing that no matter what happened today or what lies ahead, you are safe in His hands. You are a daughter of the King, forever loved and never forgotten.

Prayer
Dear God, thank You for calling me by name and claiming me as Your own. Your love is constant, and I am grateful that nothing can separate me from it. Help me to remember that my identity is found in You, and that I don't need to fear or doubt. I trust that You will continue to walk with me, showing me who I am in You.

Journaling Prompt
Reflect on how God has called you by name today. Write a letter to God, expressing how you feel about your identity in Him. How does knowing that He has redeemed you and claimed you as His own bring peace to your heart?

Day 25: God's Love Heals All Wounds

Morning Entry

Personal Note from Angel:
Good morning, beautiful soul! I hope today finds you wrapped in the warmth of God's love. Sometimes, the wounds we carry can feel too heavy to bear, but remember, God's love has the power to heal every hurt, no matter how deep. You are never too broken for His grace. Take a moment to sit with Him, knowing He understands your pain and is ready to bring healing to your heart. Let today be a fresh start, filled with hope and restoration.

Scripture (New Testament):
"He heals the brokenhearted and binds up their wounds."
– Psalm 147:3 (paraphrased in the New Testament spirit)

Poem:
In the quiet of the morning light,
God whispers healing in the night.
His love, like a gentle balm,
Soothes the ache, calms the storm.
The wounds we carry, deep and wide,
He touches with grace, arms open wide.
Every tear, every sigh,
Is seen by the One who knows why.
His mercy flows, pure and true,
Bringing peace where pain once grew.
Rest in His arms, trust His care,
For God's love heals beyond compare.

Reflection Questions (Morning):

1. How does it feel to know that God is here to heal your wounds?

2. In what ways have you experienced God's healing love in your life?

Devotional Thought:
God's love isn't just a comfort during good times; it's an anchor when we're broken. He sees every scar and every pain. The beauty of God's love is that it doesn't shy away from our brokenness but embraces it with healing hands. When we allow ourselves to rest in His love, He restores what was lost. He isn't in the business of making us perfect but of making us whole. Whatever you're facing, know that He is already at work healing and restoring you.

Prayer:
Lord, thank You for being the Healer of my heart. I bring before You my wounds and pains, trusting that You can bind them up with Your perfect love. I open myself to Your healing touch and ask that You restore every area of my life that feels broken. May Your love flood my heart today and bring me peace. In Jesus' name,

Journaling Prompt:
Take a moment to reflect on the areas in your life that need healing. Write a prayer asking God to heal your heart and bring peace where there is pain. Be specific about the areas where you need His touch today.

Evening Entry

Personal Note from Angel:
I hope today has been filled with moments of healing and peace. Remember, even when we don't see instant change, God is working within us. It's okay to take time and rest in His grace. Know that every step you take toward healing is a step toward wholeness. Let go of any burdens you're carrying tonight, and trust that God is continuing to heal you, no matter what tomorrow holds.

Scripture (Old Testament):
"He heals the broken in heart, and binds up their wounds."
– Psalm 147:3

Guided Poem:

(Finish in your own words)
I'm learning to trust that in my pain,
God's love will heal, will break every chain.
Though my heart feels heavy,
And my spirit is torn,
I know that His grace will never be worn.
With each step I take,
I feel His embrace,
Healing the wounds that time cannot erase.
And though the night seems long,
I know His love makes me strong.

Reflection Questions (Evening):

1. How did you experience God's healing love today, and how can you share that healing with someone else?

2. What is one small way you can be a source of healing or comfort to someone around you this week?

Devotional Thought:
As you rest tonight, remember that God's love is a healing force that works in ways we often can't see immediately. The process of healing might take time, but His love is constant and unchanging. Trust that He is at work in your heart, restoring what has been hurt or broken. God's love is the ultimate balm for our souls, and when we allow it to fill us, it overflows to others. Take comfort in knowing you are never alone in your journey of healing.

Prayer:
Lord, I thank You for Your healing love. As I lay down tonight, I ask that You continue to work in me, restoring the areas where I still feel broken. May Your love comfort me, bringing peace and rest to my soul. Help me to share that same healing love with others.

Journaling Prompt:
Reflect on the ways you have been healed in the past by God's love. Write about how you can help someone else experience this healing and restoration. Consider the people in your life who might need God's touch and pray for them.

Day 26: Finding Freedom in His Grace

Morning Entry

Personal Note from Angel:

Hey love, I want to remind you this morning that God's grace is truly freeing. It's not about our own strength or ability, but about His love that covers all things. Whenever we feel weighed down, His grace lifts us up. Take a deep breath and allow yourself to experience that freedom today. You are free because He loves you, and nothing can take that away. Let this truth settle in your heart as you step into your day with hope and joy.

Scripture (New Testament): "

So if the Son sets you free, you will be free indeed." – John 8:36

Poem:

In the depth of grace, I find my soul's release,
No longer bound, I walk in perfect peace.
Chains that once held me tight and cold,
Now shattered, free, no longer controlled.
His love, unearned, is my sweetest song,
In His grace, I know where I belong.
I breathe the freedom He has given,
A life of love, by grace I'm driven.
Though struggles may come, I stand tall,
For in His grace, I have it all.
A gift so free, so pure, so bright,
His grace is my constant light.

Reflection Questions (Morning):

1. How does God's grace feel to you today? In what ways have you experienced freedom in His love?

2. What areas of your life can you let go of, trusting that His grace will fill those spaces?

Devotional Thought:

Grace is one of the most powerful gifts we receive from God. It's not something we can earn or deserve, but something He freely gives because of His immense love for us. Today, think about how His grace has given you freedom – freedom from guilt, shame, and fear. His grace allows us to walk with our heads held high, knowing that no matter our struggles, His love will always be there to carry us. This morning, take a moment to embrace that freedom and feel how His grace covers every part of you.

Prayer:

Dear God, thank You for the freedom that comes from Your grace. I don't deserve it, but I am so grateful for it. Please help me to walk in that freedom each day, releasing any burdens I am carrying. Thank You for Your constant love and support. I trust in Your grace to heal me and guide me.

Journaling Prompt:

Take a moment to reflect on the ways God's grace has freed you. Write a letter to God thanking Him for His grace in your life. List the ways you've experienced freedom, whether it's freedom from past mistakes, fear, or uncertainty. Let your heart overflow with gratitude for this incredible gift

Evening Entry

Personal Note from Angel:

As the day comes to a close, I hope you feel lighter and freer. God's grace is with us not only in the good times but in every moment. I encourage you to rest tonight knowing that His grace has covered you today and will continue to sustain you. Take this peace with you as you sleep, trusting that His love will guide you through tomorrow and always.

Scripture (Old Testament):

"The Lord is merciful and gracious, slow to anger and abounding in steadfast love." – Psalm 103:8

Guided Poem:

(Finish in your own words)

I rest in the mercy of Your embrace,
A grace so deep, it fills every space.
You are slow to anger, quick to love,
Your mercy flows like the stars above.
In You, I find my comfort and peace,
From all my burdens, I find release.
Your love, unending, forever will stay,
Guiding my heart in the light of Your way.
I trust in You, my Savior and King,
For in Your grace, my heart will sing.

Reflection Questions (Evening):

1. How did you see God's grace at work in your day today?

2. How can you share God's grace with someone else tomorrow?

Devotional Thought:

As we end the day, let us remember that God's grace never ends. It's merciful, patient, and ever-abundant, offering us rest and peace. His grace allows us to sleep peacefully, knowing that He is with us in every moment. As you lay your head down tonight, trust that His mercy and love will carry you through the night and bring you peace in the morning.

Prayer:

God, thank You for Your mercy and grace. Thank You for being so patient with me and for loving me when I fall short. I rest tonight knowing that You are with me, guiding me, and giving me peace. Please help me to carry Your grace with me tomorrow and share it with those around me.

Journaling Prompt:

Take a moment to think about how you've shared God's love today. Write about one moment where you felt His grace move through you or a chance you had to share His love with someone else. Reflect on how it felt to offer grace to others and how you can continue to do so tomorrow.

Day 27: You Are His Masterpiece

Morning Entry

Personal Note from Angel:
Good morning, beautiful soul! I want you to start your day knowing that you are a masterpiece in God's eyes. No matter what the world might say or what struggles you face, God has created you with purpose and love. Remember, you are uniquely made, and He takes delight in who you are. Let that truth fill your heart today, and walk in the confidence that you are His precious creation. I'm praying for you, and I hope this day brings you closer to experiencing God's incredible love.

Scripture (New Testament):
"For we are God's masterpiece. He has created us anew in Christ Jesus, so we can do the good things he planned for us long ago." — Ephesians 2:10 (NLT)

Poem:
You are His masterpiece, perfectly designed,
In the Maker's hands, your soul entwined.
He shaped you with care, each detail refined,
With love and purpose, your heart aligned.

You shine like the stars, set high above,
A beacon of grace, a symbol of love.
In every trial, He's always near,
A masterpiece strong, free of fear.

His love will guide you through each test,
He sees you as His very best.
So walk in His grace, be who you're meant to be,
For you are His masterpiece, beloved and free.

Reflection Questions (Morning):

1. How does it make you feel to know that you are God's masterpiece?

2. In what areas of your life do you need to embrace the truth that God created you with purpose?

Devotional Thought:
God sees you as His masterpiece—perfect in His eyes. Even in the moments when we feel imperfect or lost, He still cherishes us as His work of art. Every day, He continues to shape and refine us through His love, grace, and guidance. Trust that God's plans for your life are good, and that you are exactly who He wants you to be. Lean into His love, and allow His perfect design to unfold in your life.

Prayer:
Father, thank You for creating me as Your masterpiece. Help me to see myself through Your eyes and to embrace the purpose You have for my life. I want to walk in the confidence that You designed me with love and intention. Guide me in fulfilling the good works You've planned for me.

Journaling Prompt:
Take a moment to reflect on the unique qualities and strengths God has given you. Write a letter to God, thanking Him for creating you with such intentionality and love. Ask Him to help you see your true worth and live out your purpose as His masterpiece

Evening Entry

Personal Note from Angel:
As the day winds down, I want you to remember that God's love for you doesn't end when the day ends. He is with you, always, cherishing you as His masterpiece. Rest in that truth tonight. Let go of any doubts or worries, and instead, let your heart be filled with gratitude for who you are in His eyes. Know that you are loved beyond measure.

Scripture (Old Testament):
"I will praise you because I am fearfully and wonderfully made; your works are wonderful, I know that full well." — Psalm 139:14 (NIV)

Guided Poem:

(Finish in your own words)
God made you with love, His creation so fine,
Your life is a story, uniquely divine.
You carry His light, a reflection so bright,
His hand guides you gently through day and through night.

You are a treasure, priceless and true,
A masterpiece made, just like me and you.
In His arms of love, you will always stay,
His masterpiece, forever, night and day.

Reflection Questions (Evening):

1. How did you experience God's love for you today?

2. In what ways did you share God's love with someone else today, or how can you do so tomorrow?

Devotional Thought:
You are fearfully and wonderfully made, and tonight, as you reflect on your day, remember that your worth is not defined by what the world says but by God's love for you. He sees you as His beautiful creation, full of purpose and worth. Trust that you are exactly who He wants you to be, and let His love give you peace as you rest. Tomorrow is another day to walk in His grace.

Prayer:
God, thank You for making me fearfully and wonderfully. I praise You for creating me with purpose, and I trust that You have a plan for my life. Help me to see my worth through Your eyes and share Your love with others. Thank You for always being with me.

Journaling Prompt:
As you reflect on your day, think about one way you've grown closer to God or embraced your true worth as His masterpiece. Write about it, and thank God for His love that shapes you into exactly who you were meant to be.

Day 28: God's Love Transforms You

Morning Entry

Personal Note from Angel
Good morning, beautiful soul! I hope today feels like a fresh start, a moment to embrace all the love and grace God has for you. Remember, no matter what happened yesterday, God's love is here today, ready to fill your heart and transform you. I want you to hold onto this truth—His love never changes, and it is always enough. Lean into that love today, and allow it to transform you in ways you never thought possible. You are never alone in this journey. I believe in you!

Scripture (New Testament)
"For we are God's handiwork, created in Christ Jesus to do good works, which God prepared in advance for us to do." – Ephesians 2:10

Poem
God's love, a gentle touch of grace,
Transforming hearts, renewing faith.
Through every storm and darkest night,
His love shines through, a guiding light.

No soul is too broken to be made whole,
His love restores, it heals the soul.
From pain to peace, from fear to trust,
He lifts us up, He's faithful and just.

In His embrace, we are reborn,
A brand new day, a hope to adorn.
No longer bound by past mistakes,
God's love, a gift no one can take.

Reflection Questions (Morning)

1. How do you feel God's love is transforming your heart today?

2. What is one way you can allow God's love to change the way you see yourself?

Devotional Thought
God's love is not just a comforting thought; it's a powerful force that can truly transform us. It reaches into our deepest places, healing wounds we never thought could heal. When we begin to understand that we are God's creation, that He has a purpose and a plan for us, it gives us the confidence to live boldly, knowing His love goes before us. Embrace that love today and let it guide you into the amazing things He has prepared for you. You are His masterpiece, and He is not finished with you yet.

Prayer
Dear God, thank You for the beautiful truth that Your love transforms us. I pray today that I would feel Your love in every part of my being and allow it to reshape me. Help me see myself as You see me, not defined by my past, but by the love You have for me. Fill me with the strength to share that love with others. I trust that You are always at work in me.

Journaling Prompt
Take a moment today to reflect on how God's love has transformed you in the past and how you're seeing that transformation today. Write about a moment where you felt His love make a difference in your life, and consider how you might allow that love to transform your future choices.

Evening Entry

Personal Note from Angel
As your day comes to a close, take a deep breath and remind yourself of how loved you are. The truth that God's love transforms us is something we can carry with us all day long. Reflect on the moments today where His love was evident—maybe in small ways, like a kind word, or in big moments, where you felt His presence clearly. You are worthy of His love, and I pray you feel the warmth of it as you prepare for rest tonight.

Scripture (Old Testament)
"The Lord is close to the brokenhearted and saves those who are crushed in spirit." – Psalm 34:18

Guided Poem

(Finish in your own words)
When life feels heavy, and hope seems far,
I know You're near, no matter where we are.
In every heartache, in every tear,
Your love surrounds me, You are near.

Through every struggle, You are my guide,
With You beside me, there's no need to hide.
You heal the broken, You set us free,
God's love will always, always be.

Reflection Questions (Evening)

1. How did you see God's love transforming someone else today?

2. How can you share God's love with someone who might need it tomorrow?

Devotional Thought
God's love doesn't only transform us—it equips us to help others experience that same transformation. Whether through a kind word, a listening ear, or a gentle act of compassion, we get to be conduits of His love. Tonight, as you rest, know that you are a vessel for God's love in this world, and He will continue to work through you to bring healing to those around you. Trust that His love will reach those who need it most.

Prayer
Lord, thank You for being so close to us, especially in our brokenness. I'm so grateful that Your love heals our wounds and transforms our hearts. Help me to be a vessel of Your love to those around me, especially those who are hurting or lost. Thank You for always being near and for never giving up on us. I trust in Your loving presence, tonight and always.

Journaling Prompt
Reflect on a time when you felt God's love at work in someone else's life. How did that affect you? Write about how you can be a source of that same love and healing to others, remembering that God uses us to transform the world around us.

Day 29: Embracing the Abundance of His Love

Morning Entry

Personal Note from Angel
Good morning, beautiful soul. Today, I want you to remember that God's love for you is immeasurable. It's not just a momentary feeling—it's a constant, abundant gift. I often find myself overwhelmed by the love He shows me, and I know you'll feel that same peace today. When I remind myself that His love never fails, it fills me with gratitude and hope, and I pray the same for you. No matter what you face today, His love is more than enough.

Scripture (New Testament)
"And we have come to know and believe the love that God has for us. God is love, and anyone who abides in love abides in God, and God abides in them." — 1 John 4:16

Poem
The love of God, like oceans deep,
A tide that never shall recede,
It wraps me close, it makes me whole,
A promise sealed within my soul.
When doubts arise and fears take hold,
His love is constant, bright, and bold.
I rest within His perfect grace,
A love that nothing can replace.
In every storm, His love remains,
A shelter safe from all my pains.
Abundant, endless, pure, and free,
God's love is all I'll ever need.

Reflection Questions (Morning)
1. How does knowing that God's love is endless make you feel today?

2. In what ways can you focus on God's love as a source of peace through your day?

Devotional Thought
God's love is the foundation upon which our lives are built. It is an unshakable truth, never changing and always available to us. When life feels uncertain, we can be sure that His love remains constant. This love isn't based on our actions or feelings; it is a gift from God, and it is abundant. As you embrace the abundance of His love today, let it comfort you and inspire you to share it with others.

Prayer
Lord, thank You for Your infinite love that surrounds me each day. Help me to feel the fullness of Your presence in my life. I ask that Your love fills every area of my heart and gives me peace. Teach me to trust in Your love, no matter what comes my way. I open my heart to receive Your love and share it with others

Journaling Prompt
Take a moment to write down three ways you can experience God's love today. It might be through a kind word to someone, a quiet moment of prayer, or just acknowledging His presence in your life. Write it down and let those moments fill you with joy and peace.

Evening Entry

Personal Note from Angel
As the day winds down, take a deep breath and feel the peace of knowing that God's love has been with you every step of the way. No matter what happened today, His love remains constant, and it's always there to lift you up. I pray that you feel wrapped in His arms of love, resting in the certainty that tomorrow will be filled with more of His goodness. May your heart be at peace as you close your eyes tonight.

Scripture (Old Testament)
"The Lord your God is with you, the Mighty Warrior who saves. He will take great delight in you; in His love, He will no longer rebuke you, but will rejoice over you with singing."
— Zephaniah 3:17

Guided Poem

(Finish in your own words)
The Lord, our Savior, strong and near,
In His embrace, we have no fear.
His love, a song that lifts our hearts,
A joy that never will depart.
He takes delight, He sings of me,
In His love, I am set free.
I rest in peace, I feel His grace,
And in His love, I find my place.

Reflection Questions (Evening)

1. *How did you experience God's love today?*

2. How can you share God's love with someone who might need it tomorrow?

Devotional Thought
As you reflect on today's events, remember that God's love is not bound by time or circumstance. He rejoices over you in every moment, even when you feel unworthy. This truth is a reminder that His love is abundant and that we can rest in it. We are never alone because God is with us, singing over us with joy. May His love continue to bring you peace tonight.

Prayer
God, thank You for being my constant source of love and strength. As I rest tonight, I trust in the peace that Your love brings. Help me to carry Your love into tomorrow, to share it freely with others and to always find comfort in Your arms. I know You delight in me, and I am grateful for Your everlasting love.

Journaling Prompt
Think about the ways you've experienced God's love this day. Write a letter to God expressing your gratitude for His presence in your life. Reflect on the joy and peace His love brings you, and be encouraged by how much He delights in you.

Day 30: Living a Life Overflowing with Love

Morning Entry

Personal Note from Angel
Good morning, beautiful! Today's theme is all about living a life overflowing with love, and I want you to know that you are a vessel of God's grace. As we go about our day, let's keep in mind that His love is limitless and constantly available to us. Just like a river that never runs dry, His love is meant to flow through us to others. Wherever you go today, remember that you carry His love with you, and it's meant to touch the hearts of everyone you meet. Stay open to the ways God will use you today to pour out that love!

Scripture (New Testament)
"Let all that you do be done in love." – 1 Corinthians 16:14 (ESV)

Poem
Let love be the rhythm of your heart,
A melody that never fades,
Like sunlight dancing on the ocean,
It shines in all that you create.
Through every word and every action,
Let grace and kindness guide your way,
For in the depths of love's reflection,
God's presence shines with each new day.
When you speak, let love be spoken,
When you give, give from the heart,
For in these small acts, love is woven,
And God's light shines in every part.
Your life will be a symphony,
A song of love and grace and peace,
Where God's eternal love flows free,
And all the world finds sweet release.

Reflection Questions (Morning)

1. How do you feel God's love today, and how can you share that love with others?

2. What are some small ways you can show kindness and love to those around you today?

Devotional Thought
God's love is not just something we receive; it is something we share. In 1 Corinthians 16:14, we are reminded to do everything in love. This means that every action we take, every word we speak, should be motivated by love. As we live in God's love, we become more like Him. The more we give, the more we receive, and this creates a cycle of love that overflows into the lives of others. Let today be a reminder that when we choose love, we are choosing God's will and making the world a brighter place.

Prayer
Dear God,
Thank You for Your endless love that fills my heart every day. Help me to live a life that overflows with Your love, showing kindness and grace to everyone I meet. Teach me to be more like You, loving without limits and giving from the heart. Let my actions reflect Your goodness, and may I always be a vessel of Your grace. I trust in Your love and ask You to guide me in everything I do today.

Journaling Prompt
Take a moment to think about a time when you felt God's love overflow in your life. How did it change your perspective or actions? Today, list at least three ways you can let that love overflow to others.

Evening Entry

Personal Note from Angel
As the day winds down, I want to remind you how precious you are. I hope today was filled with

little moments of love and kindness. Remember, even in the smallest acts, you can reflect God's love. Whether it was a kind word to a stranger or a quiet moment of prayer, every action done in love matters. Rest well knowing that God's love never stops flowing. He is with you, now and always.

Scripture (Old Testament)
"But the Lord will be your everlasting light, and your God will be your glory." – Isaiah 60:19 (ESV)

Guided Poem

(Finish in your own words)
The light of God shines in my soul,
His love guiding me through the night.
With every step, His grace makes me whole,
And I trust in His powerful might.
His love is the beacon I follow,
His presence a glow that never fades.
I feel His warmth, and it fills me,
A light that no darkness can invade.
And when I feel lost in the world so cold,
His light will never depart.

Reflection Questions (Evening)

1. How did you show God's love to someone today, and how did it feel?

2. What is one way you can make sure that tomorrow will be filled with love and grace?

Devotional Thought
As we reflect on today's theme, it's comforting to know that God's light never goes out. His love is everlasting, and no matter how difficult the day may have been, His grace shines brighter than any darkness. As we live in His love, we reflect His light into the world. Just as the moon reflects the sun's light, we, too, reflect God's love. Let this be a reminder to you that no matter what, His light will guide you home.

Prayer
Dear Lord,
Thank You for being my everlasting light and my glory. As I end this day, I trust in Your love to guide me through all that comes next. I am so grateful for Your constant presence in my life. Please help me to continue sharing Your love with others and to keep my heart open to You. May Your light shine through me and touch the hearts of everyone I meet.

Journaling Prompt
Reflect on a moment when you felt God's love shine brightly in your life today. Write a letter to God, thanking Him for His constant light and asking for His guidance in sharing that love with others tomorrow.

Day 31: Sharing God's Love with Others
Becoming a Vessel of Love

Morning Entry
Personal Note from Angel:
Good morning, sweet friend! Today, I want to remind you that you are a vessel of God's love. It's easy to forget that love is not just something we receive, but something we can give away freely, just as God gives it to us every day. There are so many people around us who need to feel His love, and you are the perfect person to be the light they need. As you go through your day, remember that the small acts of kindness, the words of encouragement, and even your smile can carry His love to those who need it most.

Scripture (New Testament)
"Let all that you do be done in love." – 1 Corinthians 16:14

Poem:
God's love flows through me,
A river, gentle and free.
It's not just for me to keep,
But for all to see and to seek.
I carry His love wherever I go,
In every word, in every show.
It shines in my smile, it's seen in my touch,
A whisper of peace, a comfort so much.
Let my life be a reflection so bright,
Of His endless love, His glorious light.
I'm not just a vessel, I'm a reflection true,
Of the love that God offers me and you.

Reflection Questions (Morning):

1. How do you feel God's love in your life today?

2. What small act of love can you show someone today?

Devotional Thought:
God's love is powerful, but often, we don't realize just how much of an impact it has when we let it flow through us. We can get caught up in our own struggles, but when we focus on how we can be a light to others, we start to see God's love at work in our lives in incredible ways. Whether it's a word of encouragement or a kind action, you're sharing a piece of God's heart with the world. Every time you show love, you're becoming more like Him.

Prayer:
Dear God, thank You for loving me so deeply. I ask that You help me become a vessel of Your love to those around me. Show me how to be a light in this world, and give me the courage to share Your love freely. Please use me to reflect Your grace in everything I do.

Journaling Prompt:
Take a moment to reflect on a time when someone showed you God's love in a meaningful way. How did that impact your life? How can you reflect that same love to others today?

Evening Entry

Personal Note from Angel:
As the day comes to a close, I want you to take a deep breath and feel the peace that God has given you. You've been a light in this world today, whether you realize it or not. You've shared His love, and that is something to be grateful for. As you rest tonight, know that God is working in you and through you to make a difference in the lives of others. Let that thought bring peace to your heart.

Scripture (Old Testament):
"He has shown you, O mortal, what is good. And what does the Lord require of you? To act justly and to love mercy and to walk humbly with your God." – Micah 6:8

Guided Poem:

(Finish in your own words)
God's love is merciful, kind, and pure,
It calls me to love, to be strong and sure.
I'm called to act justly, to walk in His way,
To show mercy to others every day.
In every word, in every deed,
I offer His love to those in need.
He calls me to serve with a humble heart,
And in every action, love should start.

Reflection Questions (Evening):

1. *How have you shared God's love with someone today?*

2. Who in your life could use an extra dose of God's love?

Devotional Thought:
At the end of the day, we can reflect on how well we've shared God's love with others. But even if we fall short, we can trust that God is always working in us. Every moment is a new opportunity to show love, and it doesn't take grand gestures. Sometimes, it's the little things—a listening ear, a kind word, a gentle touch—that make the biggest difference in someone's life. Let His love flow through you, and remember that He is always with you.

Prayer:
Lord, thank You for showing me how to love like You do. I ask that You continue to work in me, helping me to be a vessel of Your love in all I do. Please give me the strength and courage to show love even when it's hard. Thank You for always being with me.

Journaling Prompt:
Think about how you can continue to be a vessel of God's love tomorrow. What are some specific ways you can show love to others? Write a prayer asking God to help you be His light in the world tomorrow.

Closing Note

Dear friend,

As you reach the end of this 31-day journey, I want you to take a deep breath and know that you've just completed something incredibly powerful. You've allowed yourself to open up, reflect, and experience the healing power of God's love in ways that can truly change your heart.

Remember, this isn't the end. This is just the beginning of a new chapter—one where you are walking in the freedom of God's love, learning to trust Him with your heart, and embracing who He has called you to be. You don't have to be perfect, and you don't have to have it all figured out. You are a work in progress, and God is with you every step of the way.

Know that His love is unchanging, unshakeable, and always there for you—whether you're on a mountaintop or walking through a valley. Your journey is sacred, and God is using every moment to shape you into who He's always intended for you to be.

And if you're already feeling a change in your heart, I want to encourage you to keep going. There's so much more ahead. Stay open, stay trusting, and stay connected to the One who knows you best.

I'm excited to walk with you again in Volume 2, where we'll continue to explore how to become vessels of God's love and share that light with the world around us.

Until then, remember—God's love will always be with you. You are never alone, and you are forever cherished.

With all my love,
Angel

*If you ever want to reach out, share your thoughts, or need a prayer, I'd love to hear from you. You can email me at **angelschmidconnect@proton.me**. I'm always here for you!*

Made in the USA
Columbia, SC
29 December 2024